MAHARANA PRATAP
THE BRAVE WARRIOR

Harshikaa Udasi has chased news for most of her life, but what she has enjoyed the most is uncovering the story behind the news. Her children's stories largely dwell on the blurred lines between fact and fiction. She has written *Kittu's Very Mad Day*, *Friends Behind Walls*, *The Story Quilt* and the series *Inspiring Tales from Indian History*, among others. She has contributed to several anthologies.

Harshikaa also runs Book Trotters Collaborative through which she creates rich reading spaces for schools, mentorship programmes for educators and also a book club for children.

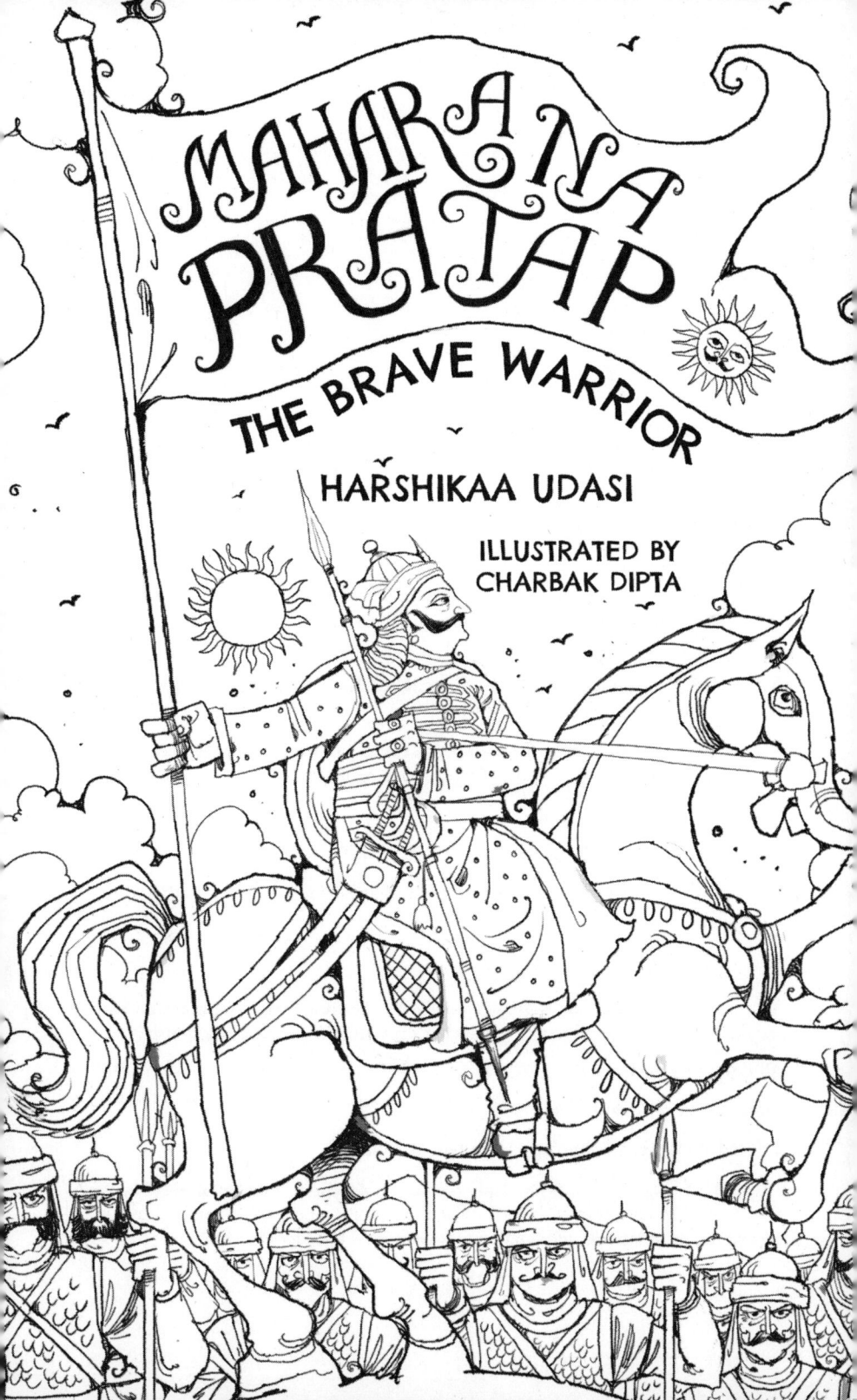

Published by Red Panda, an imprint of Westland Books, a division of Nasadiya Technologies Private Limited, in 2025

No. 269/2B, First Floor, 'Irai Arul', Vimalraj Street, Nethaji Nagar, Alapakkam Main Road, Maduravoyal, Chennai 600095

Westland, the Westland logo, Red Panda and the Red Panda logo are the trademarks of Nasadiya Technologies Private Limited, or its affiliates.

Text © Harshikaa Udasi, 2025

Illustrations © Nasadiya Technologies Private Limited, 2025

Harshikaa Udasi asserts the moral right to be identified as the author of this work.

ISBN: 9789371979597

10 9 8 7 6 5 4 3 2 1

This is a work of fiction. Names, characters, organisations, places, events and incidents are either products of the author's imagination or used fictitiously.

All rights reserved

Book design by Mukul Chand

Printed at Manipal Technologies Limited, Manipal

No part of this book may be reproduced, or stored in a retrieval system, or transmitted in any form or by any means, electronic, mechanical, photocopying, recording, or otherwise, without express written permission of the publisher.

Dedicated to those who fought and won, those who fought and lost, and those searching for the meaning of victory (and of failure)

Contents

Friends and Enemies, c.1555 1

The Boy Who Would Not Be King 9

Duties in Conflict 15

Neelo Ghodo 23

The Face-off 29

Winning Isn't Everything 34

The Promised Crown 41

Chittor's Final Celebration, c.1557 48

The Rise of Jalal 56

I Am the Ruler 62

Friendship with Benefits, c.1565 69

The Fall, 1567–1571 75

Contents

Destiny of a Maharana, c.1572 83

The Resistance 89

Snubbed, c.1573 97

Haldighati, c.1576 102

Chetak's Leap of Faith 109

The Aftermath 116

The Man Behind the Maharana, 1578–1584 125

Peace for Mewar, c.1585 131

Acknowledgements 135

Friends and Enemies, c.1555

'THINK, KEEKA. HOW WILL ONE MAN MANAGE AGAINST FOUR? They will be ferocious—the four of them, armed to the teeth with swords and spears and maces, sitting atop those massive elephants!' Bhura flung his arms around, raising himself to his full height.

Pratap ignored this overdramatic description of the puzzle, but his eyes were steadfast on the pattern Bhura had drawn in the mud. Dots represented men and crosses their choice of mount. A small cross for a horse, a large one for an elephant. Valleys and mountains were represented by 'V's and inverted 'V's. The single man was on a horse. If he managed to tackle the first soldier on the elephant, the other three would gain on him. Soon enough he would be surrounded. If he tackled everyone head on, he would be

surrounded even faster. If he startled them by coming from the opposite end, he would gain some advantage but even then, he would be surrounded. It seemed like a hopeless situation that offered no way out.

Then he smiled.

Bhura always had the trickiest puzzles for Pratap to solve. It did not matter to him that the person to whom he was putting across these challenges was Pratap Singh, prince of Mewar—soon to be the Maharana of Mewar. To him, Pratap was his closest friend. To everyone in his Bhil community, he was their *keeka*—their son. And though he was of the same age as Pratap, he couldn't resist calling his friend Keeka too.

Bhura glinted upwards. The two teenage boys were seated in the shade of the *parkota* of Kumbhalgarh fort that shielded them from the sweltering Mewar sun. The gaps in the parkota—the outer wall in a fort that acted as a protective barrier to guard against enemies—allowed them to view the entire forest and the faraway sand dunes of Marwar. He turned to Pratap. 'Keeka, if you don't come up with a solution soon...'

Pratap tilted his head and raised his eyebrows. '*Dhad!* The Bhils' style of guerrilla warfare! Bhura, I will create an illusion that I am abandoning the fight. The soldiers will believe I am completely powerless because they have outnumbered me. Then I will gallop straight into this narrow

Friends and Enemies, c.1555

mountain pass,' Pratap went on, tapping on a curve in the path leading to the mountains. 'Victory is a fickle friend; it misleads you if you're not careful—ma always says. The enemy would already be rejoicing my capture and blindly follow my lead. There, my nimble fleet of friends would be hiding with boulders and poisoned arrow tips. These would be showered on the four enemy soldiers who would enter the pass. Would that work, Bhura?' he smiled.

Bhura smiled back. 'Wrong. I never said that single soldier would be you Keeka!'

Pratap laughed. He was born right here in Kumbhalgarh and knew every nook and cranny of the fort. He also had a close group of friends who would do anything for him and for Mewar. Bhura Bhil was his closest. 'Both of us know that someday this situation could be a possibility, and I could be standing alone against not four but even four thousand, Bhura. That's when all your tactics and puzzles are going to help me,' Pratap said, placing his hand on his friend's shoulder.

'Wrong once again! Keeka, you will never be alone. I will always be by your side,' proclaimed Bhura, dramatically pulling out an imaginary arrow from the quiver, placing it on his imaginary bow and pulling the bowstring.

'Be by my side? Yes, that you will. But I think you have an even more significant duty towards Mewar. Do you want to

know what that is?' Pratap prodded his friend mischievously but the naïve Bhura did not realise it.

'What? What is it? Is it taking care of Kumbhalgarh? O Vaaghdevi!' Bhura's eyes sparkled with excitement.

'Well, we need someone to tell our stories—of valour, of war, of strategies, of weaknesses—to our people. So that they learn from our best moves and avoid our mistakes. So that they are filled with pride at being Mewaris. And who better than you for telling stories and dramatizing situations? Remember the other day, maiya was telling us about the dance-drama festival Gavari? You are perfect for the job!'

With that, Pratap jumped up and dashed towards the Bhairon Pol, the first gate that led inwards to the humungous Kumbhalgarh fort. The two friends had literally grown up in the ravines and forests of the region and could navigate their way on foot. They could both run down to Bhairon Pol in even lesser time than a horse would take. 'You're just a storyteller; you won't be able to beat me!' he shouted, speeding towards the gate. Bhura, though taken aback by Pratap's flash run, quickly rose to his feet.

'I am your teacher, Keeka! I will be thrilled if you defeat me!' he said.

Pratap darted across the uneven path that stretched endlessly. His friend was close on his heels. But soon, at a hairpin curve in the path, Pratap disappeared. Bhura leaned

over the parkota to check. *There is no chance that Keeka could have fallen over*, he thought, and continued to run towards Bhairon Pol. Soon enough, he heard a voice.

'Bhuraaaa!'

He could see his Keeka waving from the gate. It took him a long time to reach there. 'Okay, what do you know about this route that I don't?' he said, bending forward to catch his breath.

Pratap was lying down on the ground—something he loved doing. 'Yesterday, I discovered a set of steps completely camouflaged by the shrubbery. They disappear under the mountain and emerge close to Bhairon Pol. The path is dark and steep. It has a steady trickle of water from its walls but it's a quick one,' he revealed.

Bhura nodded in admiration. Their Keeka was fit to be the Maharana. As their village headman often said, he would bring glory to Mewar.

Pratap knew the look that Bhura gave him. He had almost read his mind. 'Ma always tells me about the history of our family—how my ancestors always stood for what is right and how they fought to retain the independence and respect of Mewar. But what a price we have paid, Bhura. We have constantly been on the battlefield. There have been *jauhars*, when our women walked into flames to protect their honour. And the *sakas*—those desperate last battles when the men of Mewar rode out to die, dressed in saffron, knowing

Friends and Enemies, c.1555

they would never return. It rattles my soul. I wish to bring an end to it all. I wish to establish Mewar's name high up in the sky—so high that no one can ever touch it again.'

'And you will, without a doubt,' said Bhura, as he reached out for the small bundle he had tied to his waist.

'Mewar has attracted Afghanis and Mughals over the centuries. It is rich in minerals and blessed by the mighty Aravalli. Its devious landforms and dense forests make it a formidable challenge for enemies to acquire it. But that is the attraction too. They want Mewar because they know it will never let them down. It is strategically and commercially important. I wish I could right away wipe off all those who cast an evil eye on my Mewar!' Pratap's fists were tightly curled around two stones he held.

'That day will also come, but hold that anger within and unleash it when the time is right. Now answer this very important question,' said Bhura.

'Another question? I am ready. Bring it on,' said Pratap, turning to his friend.

'What has my mai sent for you in this?' Bhura asked, pointing to the cloth bundle.

Pratap was thrilled. Talking about Mewar and bounding about the fort with his friend all the afternoon had left him famished. 'If mai has sent something,' he said, taking a deep sniff, 'it is definitely mawa kachori!'

Bhura nodded. The two friends sat next to each other hungrily munching on the delicious mix of milk, ghee and khoya.

The year was 1555. Pratap was just fifteen years old then. But far away from Mewar, in Punjab's Kalanaur, destiny had chosen his arch enemy. The young Akbar, only thirteen, was waiting to be crowned. Theirs was an enmity that would span decades and would have reams written about it. Pratap did not know yet but he had been preparing all along for this face-off. And Bhura and the Bhils were making sure that he would succeed.

The Boy Who Would Not Be King

'JAI SHREE EKLINGNATHJI, MA!' PRATAP GREETED HIS MOTHER early the next morning. Jaiwanta Bai was ready for her puja.

'You've woken up well before sunrise, Pratap. *Jai Shree Eklingnathji*,' his mother replied, surprised. 'Did you sleep well? Or were you dreaming again—about something you're waiting to tell me?' she asked, smiling. Her only son was as much a warrior as he was a dreamer.

Only yesterday, his guru had told her how Pratap had aced at swordsmanship.

'Maharani Jaiwanta Baiji, Kunwar Pratap has become extremely good with his footwork. He never misses his target and can land a counterattack before his opponent can come to his senses. This morning, he managed to outwit me twice,' Guru Avadhuta had said, pride clearly reflecting on

his face. 'I have fought alongside Maharana Sangha and if I have seen such lightning moves by anyone other than him it is by Pratap. I sense he is the future of Mewar.' Jaiwanta Bai had smiled with quiet pride—more so when the guru had spoken of the kunwar's vision for his motherland.

'He often speaks of this recurring dream—standing on the battlefield, with both his grandfather, Maharana Sangha, and his father, Maharana Udai, right beside him. Together they fight an unseen enemy and unfurl the Suryavanshi flag, chanting 'Jai Mewar!' the guru had said.

'Ma! Why do you get lost in thought so often? And how did you know I had another dream? Yes, I want to tell you what happened!' Pratap said eagerly, brimming with excitement.

His mother ran her fingers lovingly through his hair. 'I'll hear you out—but on the way to the temple. Now quickly take a bath. Let's go together today.'

Mondays for Jaiwanta Bai began with prayers at the Neelkanth Mahadev temple of Kumbhalgarh. She would slowly make her way down the fort path well before sunrise. Every Monday—on the way down, at the temple, and all the way back—she would repeat just one prayer: *Hey Shree Eklingnathji! Let Pratap be the king Mewar deserves. Let him bring glory to Mewar.*

As the eldest queen of Udai Singh, she was deeply connected to the people of Mewar and understood what

The Boy Who Would Not Be King

they longed for. She also sensed what Pratap wished to do for his motherland. But she was keenly aware of the politics brewing in Gogunda, not far from Kumbhalgarh. Udai Singh was currently spending time there with his favourite queen, Dheer Bai. Rumour had it that if she had her way, Pratap—despite being the eldest—would not be the next king. Dheer Bai wished to see her own son, Jagmal, barely a year old, on the throne.

On the way to the temple, Pratap narrated his dream in great detail.

'I was on the furthest hill of the Aravalli—there,' he said, pointing into the distance. 'I heard the drumbeats signalling danger. Then I saw the central flame light up. I looked around. How could I come back to Kumbhalgarh and fight the enemy? I thought all was lost. Just then, out of nowhere, a majestic blue horse appeared. I mounted it, and suddenly he flew me over the thirteen hills! *Flew*, Ma, flew! I was soaring like a giant bird over the forests and hills. It brought me right back here. Then I woke up. I wanted to shut my eyes again and see what happened next, but I couldn't.'

Hey Shree Eklingnathji, thank you, his mother whispered, folding her hands. 'Pratap, to see a horse in your dreams is a very good omen! It symbolises success and ambition. I am certain you are blessed.'

Pratap beamed.

Then she pulled his nose and added, 'And what you missed seeing in your dream—I can complete it for you. You fought the enemy alongside Maharana Sangha and your baapu, and you won the battle!'

'Ma! Are you teasing me now?' Pratap protested. 'But only you understand me and my dreams so well. I'm certain we were fighting to keep invaders off Chittor.'

The queen winced.

Chittor had borne deep wounds—first in 1303 by Delhi's Sultan Alauddin Khilji, and later by Gujarat's Sultan Bahadur Shah twice between 1532 and 1535. If that wasn't enough, the land had been plagued by internal conflict after Maharana Sangha's death.

It was only shortly after Pratap's birth that Udai Singh had regained control of Chittor and its fort. Mewar had rejoiced; the priests had proclaimed that the newborn had changed the region's fortunes. But that joy had been short-lived.

Pratap had barely turned five when Udai Singh had surrendered the keys of Chittor to the Afghan ruler Sher Shah. It had been a tactical move to protect Mewar's people, with a plan to reclaim the fort later. Still, the pain of watching invaders occupy Chittor was deeper than any defeat.

Would Pratap be able to heal those wounds—perhaps even avenge them?

The Boy Who Would Not Be King

At the temple, the priest began the rituals. Jaiwanta Bai asked Pratap to light the diyas at the shivalinga and around the temple. As dawn broke, the stillness of the temple, the fragrance of flowers, the glow of a hundred lamps, and the soothing chant of prayers created a magical, mesmerising moment. Yet, the mother's heart sensed something was not quite right. Something that only the Supreme Ruler of Mewar, Parameshwara Maharaj Shree Eklingnathji, could set straight.

After the prayers, the two began their walk back to the top of the fort in silence. The morning sun bathed Kumbhalgarh in a soft light, its cream and grey stone glistening like a pearl. A cool breeze drifted through the Aravalli forests. Pratap stopped and took his mother's hand.

'Sometimes, Ma, I wonder if my dreams are merely dreams—or is there something more to them?'

Jaiwanta Bai was taken aback by the suddenness of his words. He had echoed what had been troubling her ever since Dheer Bai had earned the favour of Udai Singh. Jaiwanta Bai also knew it would be unwise to dismiss the rumours.

'Wh-why do you say that, Pratap?' she stammered, trying to mask her unease. 'I must be getting old. This walk up and down is making me pant and gasp for breath.'

'Ma, there's no use denying it. I understand you want to protect me from the harsh truth, but it is as clear as day

from night. Baapu may be compelled not to choose me as his successor. And if that happens—just like Ramachandra—I will walk away. I, too, am a Suryavanshi.'

Duties in Conflict

AT GOGUNDA, A SHORT DISTANCE AWAY FROM KUMBHALGARH, Udai Singh was in deep thought. It had been over a decade since he agreed to the Chittor truce and it often kept him restless. Had he made the right decision by offering Chittor to the Afghan, Sher Shah, on peace terms?

He had managed to push the Afghans out eventually, but Chittor was always open to threats. Sher Shah's attack made him realise the need for other secure capitals for Mewar. He had learnt not to rely only on Chittor. Now, he kept moving between Gogunda and Kumbhalgarh, but he knew there was need for more. So far, what was working to protect his kingdom was Gogunda's proximity to the Kumbhalgarh fort. Kumbhalgarh had never tasted defeat and it was the pride of the Mewaris. He could move swiftly between these two forts if there was a sudden attack, and this swiftness was his strength.

Having weighed the pros and cons of the Chittor treaty, and seemingly satisfied with his policy of establishing new capitals, he turned to Rawat Kishandas, his minister and one of his closest aides.

'Rawat Kishandasji, please arrange to begin work on our new capital on the land we have chosen near Lake Pichola. It will be perfect for our new seat of power. With the blessings of the saint, Goswami Prem Giriji Maharaj, and the presence of natural water and mineral resources, this city will serve Mewar well,' he announced.

'Yes, Maharanaji. I will make arrangements for the work to commence immediately. With your permission, I would like to suggest something as well,' said his minister.

Udai Singh nodded.

'Your ancestor, Rana Lakha, was a man of great foresight. Lake Pichola, near which our new capital will come up, was made by him. He understood that, in times of natural challenges or enemy attacks, Mewar faced the threat of water scarcity. Lake Pichola was created so that rainwater could be stored and used throughout the year. My suggestion is that you should also create another lake for the same purpose.'

The Maharana thought about this for a long time. Then he spoke. 'Rana Lakha was a visionary. Also, Rawatji, learning from our enemies is essential. As much as I carry hatred in my heart for Sher Shah for taking on Chittor, I have seen what he did to the land. The wells and embankments he built

have benefitted the people immensely. Your suggestion is very valuable. Let us build a lake.'

'Thank you. I will have work started on Udai Sagar as well as the new capital,' he smiled. Then he hesitated slightly. 'Maharanaji, if I may, there is one more matter I would like to bring to your attention,' he said.

'Never hesitate to tell me the state of affairs,' the king said sharply.

'It's the Chauhans of Vagarh. I have been receiving disturbing reports from the region. There have never been clearly defined borders. But sometimes, the goats taken to graze by our goatherds stray close to the Som river, into their territory. Of late, several of our goatherds have been harassed by Vagarh soldiers. In the last few months, I have personally observed many Vagarh traders entering our markets without identifying themselves. This has never happened before, and it raises suspicions about their real intentions. It is a signal, Maharanaji. We must be prepared.'

'Hmm. We must. I will speak to the council soon. What's the news of Maharani Jaiwanta Bai and Kunwar Pratap?'

'They are well protected, Maharanaji. Around thousand soldiers are guarding Kumbhalgarh as we speak, and Rawat Sangaji is there too. But what the people of Kumbhalgarh are most happy about is having Kunwar Pratap near them. Kunwarji is not only a brave heart but also skilled in military tactics and strategy. Rawat Sangaji himself has spoken very

Duties in Conflict

highly of him. He said that as long as Kumbhalgarh has Kunwar Pratap, everyone will be safe.' Rawat Kishandas' eyes gleamed with pride.

'Proceed with the new capital, Rawat Kishandasji. We will call the new place Udaipur,' replied the Maharana.

Rawat Kishandas was an intelligent man. As many said, he was someone who could count the feathers of a bird in flight. The Maharana's complete ignoring of Pratap's praise confirmed his doubts about the king's attitude towards his eldest and most capable son. Udai Singh was slowly distancing himself from Pratap.

But Rawat Kishandas was not one to betray his emotions to the Maharana. 'Udaipur is the perfect name for your new capital! Centuries will remember you for this,' he said and left the court. 'And if you do what I think you might, then centuries will remember you for that act too,' he muttered under his breath as he walked away.

'Keeka? Kunwar? You? Here?' Bhura wasn't sure if he was dreaming or if his friend, the prince of the state, was actually standing at his door.

'What has startled you so much, Bhura? And who is this Kunwar?' A mischievous smile spread across Pratap's face.

Bhura realised what he had called his friend and looked away, embarrassed. But he soon found his voice. 'I wasn't expecting you here, that's all. My house is very far from the fort. How did you make it here?' he asked.

'I have an excellent teacher, you see. He's been teaching me to look for signs and even taught me directions based on the movement of the sun. Do you want to know who he is?' laughed Pratap.

Bhura threw back his head in mock pride. 'That won't be necessary.'

'To answer your question—I followed the path most walked until the sun was right over my head. I remembered that my teacher told me he lived near the largest dhak tree, which is now in full bloom. See—*jungle ki aag!*' He pointed to the large tree ablaze with bright orange flowers.

Bhura hugged his friend. Nearby, other Bhils gathered to see their Keeka. They bowed to him and he greeted them with folded hands. Bhura's father, who was busy cutting wood and tying it into neat bundles, hurried to the house and welcomed Keeka into the village. Bhura's mother was harvesting bark from the khadira tree. Her Ayurvedic medicines were famous in Kumbhalgarh fort too. On seeing him, she gave him a warm hug.

'Keeka, if I had known you're coming I would have made something you would have loved!'

Duties in Conflict

'Your mawa kachori was delicious, Mai! We had it just two days ago. Today, I came to meet you all because we will be leaving for a new place for some time,' Pratap said.

He looked at his friend. Bhura looked disappointed.

The two friends walked into the jungle.

'You know how it is with us, Bhura. I was born here, then I moved to Chittor. After Chittor was snatched from us, I came back while baapu and Rani Dheer Bai maiya stayed in Gogunda. Now, he wants us all to move again.'

Bhura stayed silent, looking ahead.

'You've taught me this, haven't you? Never get too comfortable in one place. What was that' you used to say?' Pratap tried to recall.

'Travel fast, travel light
Travel at night, stay out of sight...'

The two boys chorused the rest.

'Light fleet, nimble feet
Strike hard, leave fast
Mouth shut, eyes sharp
Ears open... your trap's woven!'

Bhura hugged Pratap. He was going to miss his friend, but he couldn't stop him from becoming what life had destined him to be—the Maharana of Mewar.

'I've often wondered whether I should say this. But since I don't know what the situation will be when I see you next, I must speak. Keeka, forgive me for saying this,' said Bhura.

'What is it?' said Pratap, placing a hand on his friend's shoulder. 'You can tell me anything, you know that.'

Bhura closed his eyes, then looked squarely at his friend.

'If you ever have to choose between your duty as a son and your duty as a ruler, please choose the second.'

'I—I don't know...' Pratap hesitated.

'Keeka!' Bhura's mother called out. 'Come here. I've made *kodo ki roti* for you. In your palace, you'll never get to eat these grass rotis!'

Neelo Ghodo

CHITTOR. BEAUTIFUL CHITTOR.

Pratap's joy had known no bounds when he discovered that they were moving back to Chittor. Even though his heart was in Kumbhalgarh, it was Chittor that always beckoned him. When he was barely five years old, Udai Singh had made the difficult decision to share Chittor with the Afghans. Sher Shah had taken over and given his deputy, Shams Khan, absolute power over the city. However, by a stroke of unexpected luck, Sher Shah died the very next year, and pushing Shams Khan out of Chittor had been an easy task for Udai Singh. Even so, the Maharana and the royal family did not stay long in Chittor. They kept moving across the various capitals he had built.

But this year, the royals were back in their ancestral palace and fort. It was the day before Dussehra when they arrived in the city. Dussehra was a very special festival for

the Suryavanshis, who celebrated the victory of their Ram over Raavan. Lit-up Chittorgarh was a treat to behold. Flowers adorned the doorways and hallways. The whole city was filled with the aroma of festive food—*dal baati churma* and *malpua rabdi*. To ensure everyone's safety, Udai Singh had spread his family across Mewar, while he remained in Gogunda with Dheer Bai and their son, Jagmal. But today was the first time in years that the entire family had come together for the festival.

'Isn't it wonderful to see everyone so happy, Shakti? When was the last time we spoke to each other? I pray this is how my Mewar remains for years to come!' said Pratap. He was sitting next to his half-brother, Shakti Singh, son of Sajja Bai.

'My Mewar? Is it not *our* Mewar, Daada?' Shakti Singh responded quickly.

Pratap looked at Shakti wearily. This brother of his always managed to pick a fight with him, whether over trivial matters or more serious ones.

'Ours, it is, Shakti. But are *you* Mewar's? I said *my* Mewar because I belong to Mewar completely. I have dedicated my life—and my death—to my motherland.'

Shakti pressed his lips tight. 'And what if Mewar does not want you?' he retorted.

'That shall never be. You'll see tomorrow,' Pratap said with a frown, picking up his sheath and shield.

For centuries, Mewaris had worshipped their weapons on Dussehra during the Shastra puja. Pratap and Shakti, the two eldest princes, were preparing for a special performance the next morning—a face-off that all the people of Chittor and nearby villages were expected to attend. Rawat Sanga, who was in charge of the princes' training, wanted to test the brothers' skills.

Before Shakti could respond with a proper retort, the boys were distracted by a great commotion near the main gate, Ram Pol. They stood on tiptoe, craning their necks to see what was causing such a ruckus. They soon realised it was not an 'it'—it was *them*. Ten magnificent horses, neighing, as they made their way through the crowds. The people were applauding. Shakti and Pratap looked on in awe. It was quite a splendid sight.

However, not all ten horses trotted in a single line. Pratap's eyes fell on one that walked well ahead of the others, as though it wanted to chart its own path. He wasn't running—he was elegantly galloping. His coat was a unique hue of blue, with a wild silvery mane. As he came closer, Pratap noticed his sturdy legs and steady gait. Not ambling—very straight. His gaze was intense, as though he could pierce one's soul with his large, expressive eyes. Pratap remembered a book he had read—*Shalihotra*—on selecting and nurturing the finest stallions. This one seemed to be the very picture of perfection, straight out of its pages.

Everyone had gathered to see the horses. Bharmal Kawadia, the prime minister of Udai Singh, presented them as a gift to the Maharana. Bharmal shared a deep bond with the royal Sisodia family. He had been a loyal ally of Maharana Sangha as well, serving as one of his key generals.

'This is such a special gift for Ashwa puja, Bharmalji,' Udai Singh said, thanking his prime minister. In Mewar, horses were worshipped on navami, the ninth night of Navratri, in gratitude for their partnership with warriors.

'It is an honour, Maharanaji, to serve Mewar—our traditions, our people and our brave rulers,' Bharmal replied, as the horses were prepared for the ritual.

Pratap stood next to his father as the Ashwa puja was underway.

'Pratap, the best horse among these will be either yours or Shakti's, depending on who wins tomorrow's face-off. From what Rawat Sangaji has told me, your skills are superior to your brother's. What do you think?'

'I think Shakti is a skilled warrior, Baapu,' he replied. 'Yet, since my guruji has taught me that a true prince never hesitates to state the truth plainly, I must say this—my brother needs to work harder. He needs to perfect the stability and calmness that a Mewari warrior must have.'

'And you? Do you claim to have all these qualities?' his father asked, smiling.

'Guruji says that one remains a learner for life. I am learning, Baapu. All I can say is that I am a good student,' he smiled back.

For a moment, Pratap did not care whether he would become the future ruler of Mewar, or whether his father loved his brothers—Jagmal, Shakti, or any of the others—more than him. He simply wanted that moment to last; such moments with his father were rare now.

For a moment, even Udai Singh pushed aside the thought that had taken root in his mind. Jagmal as king? That seemed laughable now. He wanted to forget it. He could see Mewar's future standing before him in the form of Pratap. He could see its glory.

He nodded with satisfaction. 'I wish you the best, Pratap. For tomorrow. And forever.'

Taking his father's blessings, Pratap cast one final look at the *neelo ghoda* he had chosen and returned to his chamber.

The Face-off

A WINDING, SNAKE-LIKE CROWD LINED UP AT RAM POL EARLY the next morning. People from not just Chittor but all the nearby villages and towns had gathered to see the royal family—especially the two royal princes. The village gossip mills were working overtime.

'Kunwar Pratap fights just like Maharana Sangha, I've heard!' said one.

'He's just fifteen, but he's taller than his father!' exclaimed another.

'Not simply taller—I've seen him! He must be at least *teen gaz* tall. He has a full-grown moustache too, just like the Maharana!' added a third.

Had Pratap heard any of these comments, he would have definitely worried about his yet non-existent moustache—and his height, which was certainly not greater than his

father's! The comparison with his grandfather would have made him nervous, too; those were big shoes to fill.

However, away from the street talk and all distractions, Pratap was readying himself for the freestyle duel with his brother, Shakti. His sword was at the ready, and he carried a quiver of arrows and his bow, for he excelled in both archery and swordsmanship. Dressed in a white robe, he arrived at the grounds where the contest was to be held. Shakti was dressed in a red robe, the contrast allowing spectators to distinguish them easily.

Jaiwanta Bai and Sajja Bai watched from afar as their sons faced each other.

'Isn't this something we could do without, Jaiwanta Jiji?' Sajja Bai asked the eldest queen. 'I wonder what good comes of putting our young children through this. Brother against brother?'

Jaiwanta Bai calmed her gently. 'As mothers, it's difficult to watch, Behna. But this is what our dynasty is known for—its valour and skill. These qualities will serve them on the battlefield. So, consider this a training ground. And remember, the rules do not allow either of them to hurt the other. Watch it like a game of skill and you won't be upset.'

'Yes, watch it as a game,' a third voice rose behind them. They recognised Dheer Bai at once.

'After all, nothing comes from nothing. Nothing ever could,' she said cryptically.

The Face-off

'You are an ace at puzzles, dear Dheer. For today, at least, put them aside and watch Maharanaji's sons. Have a seat,' said Jaiwanta Bai.

'Sure, Jaiwanta Jiji. If only my Jagmal were old enough to participate! That would make me very happy,' she said, glancing at the queen.

Jaiwanta Bai, not one to be drawn into a war of words, held her peace.

Just then, the drums were sounded. Rawat Sanga called both princes to the centre and asked them to seek the blessings of Shree Eklingnathji. He then announced the final task of the face-off and its rules.

'Kunwar Pratap and Kunwar Shakti, the first among you to shoot an arrow exactly at this post will be declared the winner. At no point during the contest are you to hurt each other. If blood spills, you will be disqualified. If your weapon falls, you may retrieve it or choose another. Are these rules understood?'

Both nodded.

'Now repeat after me—*Jai Shree Eklingnathji!*'

The boys chanted in unison, '*Jai Shree Eklingnathji!*' With that, he declared the contest open.

The two swords clanged first.

Shakti knew his strength—his fury would carry him through this face-off. And fury, he had in plenty. He was younger than Pratap and had always lived in his shadow. His

father never thought highly of him, and his mother rarely recommended him either. Shakti channelled all his pent-up anger into the attack.

Pratap shielded himself from the incoming blows. He was swift, focused, and not prone to anger. Turning in one swift move, he jabbed at Shakti's armour, making him stagger. Shakti's response was slow. Before he could recover, Pratap swung his sword around twice and managed to pierce through Shakti's robe.

'Daada!' Shakti screamed, shocked.

'I haven't hit you, Shakti. Fight!' Pratap shouted back.

The spectators were in stunned silence.

'See? Just like Maharana Sangha! Told you so,' an old warrior whispered to his companion.

On the field, Shakti lunged again, and this time Pratap bent backwards. Shakti lost his balance—and his sword—and fell to the ground. Pratap seized the moment, picked up his bow, and drew an arrow. His eyes focused on the post, he pulled the bowstring back and let the arrow fly.

'Excellent, Pratap!' Udai Singh applauded from the viewing area, and the crowd erupted in cheer.

Pratap helped his brother to his feet, then rushed to his parents for their blessings. He looked at his father expectantly.

Udai Singh patted him and said, 'Your guruji was not wrong. You do have lightning moves, Pratap. That was

The Face-off

exceptional. And I do remember what I said last night. Which horse would you like for yourself?'

Unable to hide his excitement, Pratap replied at once, '*Neelo ghodo*, Baapu!'

Rana Udai was pleased with his choice.

The *sanjab* Marwari horse was brought to the young prince. Pratap gently caressed its face and looked into its large eyes.

'I shall name you Chetak. He who knows where he is going. He who knows what his responsibility is. He who is as thoughtful as his rider. Be my partner forever, Chetak!'

Winning Isn't Everything

A YEAR HAD PASSED SINCE THE ROYAL FAMILY HAD SHIFTED to Chittor, and Pratap was now sixteen. His agility, and his sharp, precise responses on the field, were unmatched—as was his understanding of political alliances.

'See these areas, Pratap. This is where Mewar sits. It is surrounded by Marwar, Malwa and Gujarat. There are no walls between these, and within our Mewar there are smaller territories that run independently. The invasions Mewar faces are mostly from the Afghans from Delhi, the Mughals, and the Sultans of Gujarat,' said Guru Avadhuta, Pratap's teacher in ethics, morality, war strategy and swordsmanship.

'Baapu and Rawat Sangaji were speaking about a rising problem with Vagarh, which lies on the border of our Mewar and Gujarat,' Pratap said, studying the map intently.

'Yes, Maharanaji will need to decide about Vagarh soon. Heavy lies the head that wears the crown. Remember,

Winning Isn't Everything

Pratap, a ruler always has to decide three things. First, who are our friends? Second, who are our enemies? And finally, who are we willing to befriend to fight those enemies?' said his guru.

'Alliances. Like how we have always united against Afghani and Mughal invaders,' said Pratap.

'Yes, that's right. It is a political strategy—either to maintain peace between powerful rulers or to increase one's strength against an invader. Alliances are often formed through marriages between different clans; in fact, that is the foundation of the closest alliances. Your ancestors have done this to bring more strength to Mewar. However, now several kings—even of the Rajputana—have begun accepting marriage alliances with the Mughals. One thing many rulers forget while making such important decisions is to ask: is this the right thing to do?' his guru said, looking up at him.

'But there is no rule book that says what is right and what is wrong. So how is a ruler to decide?' Pratap asked, puzzled.

'That's when you turn to the pages of history. Has anyone faced a similar situation before? What did they do? What happened as a result? And then you also think with your head and your heart. Never focus on short-term gains. Always ask what effect your decision will have on the future. Most importantly—will it be fair? Will it hurt someone's honour? These are the things a ruler must consider,' Guru Avadhuta explained.

Pratap looked at him and asked, 'So baapu leaving Chittorgarh when I was small—that wasn't a wrong decision?'

Guru Avadhuta nodded. 'I'm glad you asked this. Who is to say what was right or wrong? On that day, in those circumstances, I am sure the Maharana made the best decision he could. Perhaps you or I would have chosen differently. But it wasn't our decision to make. You know that within the very next year, Maharanaji's destiny brought him back to Chittorgarh. When the time is right, things fall into place. During difficult times, what remains in your control is your decision to keep trying.'

Pratap had a faraway look in his eyes.

Guru Avadhuta continued, 'Pratap, no king has escaped the burden of difficult decisions. And if you ever face a similar moment, remember to choose long-term wins over short-term gains.'

'So winning is everything?' Pratap asked.

'Yes. When you are fighting for your people's safety, your self-respect and your independence, winning *is* everything. But the definition of victory—that is for you to decide.'

~

After a long day of studying Sanskrit, Pratap stepped out of his home. Besides his own chamber with a wooden bed, there was a room for his caretakers, one for his books and

Winning Isn't Everything

weapons, and an open front yard where he took his lessons. There, under a covered shed, stood his partner—Chetak.

Pratap had insisted that Jaiwanta Bai should not accompany him to Bassi, where his father had arranged this accommodation.

'I would like you to live among our people and understand what they need, Pratap,' his father had said.

A hush had fallen over the court.

'Maharanaji, is it wise to have Kunwar Pratap live in a village, outside the protection of the palace?' Rawat Sanga had ventured to ask. But the Maharana would hear none of it.

'I will leave right away, Baapu. I only ask for permission to move freely across Chittorgarh and its neighbouring areas,' Pratap had said. If he was to live independently, he wanted complete freedom.

With permission granted, he had moved to a small village on the edge of the forest near Chittorgarh. His gurus came frequently to Bassi for his lessons. Occasionally, he received a message from his father, summoning him to join small expeditions across the kingdom. He saw his mother sometimes. She would come not only to visit him but to guide him in his education—and always brought his favourite dishes.

But by now, Pratap was skilled at identifying and eating the right foods from the forest. He had learnt to manage

with whatever he had, especially when provisions from the palace were delayed. He enjoyed sharing food with his caretakers and never hesitated to eat what they ate.

Pratap smiled and spoke to Chetak. 'Chetak, baapu wanted me to live with our people. What could be better than this? Do you like it here, or do you prefer the royal stables of Chittorgarh?'

The steed neighed and nudged his master's face in response.

'Me, you ask? I love it here. I've got as good a bed as anyone could want. I have one of my best friends beside me. And I know maiya is safe in the palace. What else does one need?'

The sound of approaching horsemen caught Pratap's attention. A small troop was headed his way, led by a messenger from Chittorgarh.

'And look there, Chetak—royal messengers again!' he laughed.

The lead messenger dismounted and hurried to him.

'Kunwar Pratap, Maharanaji has sent a note for you. And a contingent of fifty soldiers,' he said.

Pratap frowned. An army of his own? Was his father entrusting him with a battle? He read the letter:

Pratap,

Jai Shree Eklingnathji Maharaj!

Winning Isn't Everything

The Chauhans of Vagarh have been creating trouble, as you know. I trust you to show them not to meddle with Mewar. My men on horseback will accompany you. Start at once.

Maharana Udai Singh

'Signed as Maharana—not baapu,' Pratap thought. 'But he has seen in me what I've always hoped he would.' He smiled.

'This will be done,' he said, turning to the messenger. 'Tell Maharanaji that I will meet him when I return.'

'Are you leaving now, Kunwar Pratap?' the messenger asked. 'I shall inform Maharanaji accordingly.'

'That is for me to decide. If I am to lead, I will do it my way,' said Pratap, thinking of Bhura. Then, moving to the soldiers, he asked, 'So, which one of you is the fastest and the sharpest?'

Without hesitation, a young man stepped forward. 'Kunwar, I am fast, my horse is sure-footed, and my ears are very sharp. Tell me what you need. I can do it.'

'Good. Get me all the information you can about the Chauhans' movements. Observe closely near the Som river and anywhere else you spot anyone from Vagarh. Keep your ears open and your mouth shut. Not a soul should know we're about to strike. Understood? What's your name?'

'Tej Lal, Kunwar. It will be done. I'll return in two days.'

'May Shree Eklingnathji be with you, Tej,' said Pratap, assured that this young soldier had the fire and skill for the task. Then he turned to the others.

'If you want to fight by my side, if you want Mewar to win, if you love your motherland, then etch these rules into your heart and mind:

Travel fast, travel light,
Travel at night, stay out of sight.
Light fleet, nimble feet,
Strike hard, leave fast.
Mouth shut, eyes sharp,
Ears open ... your trap's woven!'

The Promised Crown

THE MOOD IN THE ROOM WAS TENSE. SHAKTI PACED ABOUT furiously. 'This is not to be my fate, ma,' he said aloud. His mother, Sajja Bai, stood close, trying to pacify him. 'Look, Shakti, I understand your anger but there is no justification for your behaviour. You are not the eldest-born son of Maharanaji. So, there is no way—' she was interrupted angrily.

'So Jagmal isn't either!' Shakti threw a tantrum. 'But Ranima Dheer Bai is making every effort to put him on the throne. She doesn't care if Pratap daada is the rightful heir. You aren't doing anything to help me, ma.'

The queen's eyes glowered. 'Listen, Shakti. This is no way to talk to your mother. Secondly, I don't stand by what Dheer Bai is doing. It's unethical and it is not in favour of Mewar. You need to understand that your mother is

not like her. I will never do anything that goes against my motherland,' her voice quivered.

It didn't matter that her son was furious. She was a woman of principles and understood the underlying politics of Mewar very well too.

Shakti hardly expected his mother to respond aggressively. She usually didn't. He steadied himself and sat on her cot.

'Good. Now listen and try to understand me,' said Sajja Bai. 'History is never written only about the rulers but also about those who supported them. In fact, sometimes those who support the cause of the kingdom, the guiding principles of the kingdom, get a glorified space in history."

Shakti was unconvinced and he averted her eyes, anger still boiling within.

'Alright,' she said, knowing fully that he hadn't calmed down. 'Lie down on my lap like you used to as a child.' Hesitantly, Shakti did so. It felt awkward as a teenager but the warmth of his mother's lap was comforting.

'Hmm, now think about Panna Dai. Only to safeguard Mewar, didn't she place her son to die and move your father out of the chamber when his uncle Banveer attacked him? Think about Kunwar Chunda. He was supposed to inherit the throne. But you know that he gave it up as his mother Hansa Bai wanted her son on the throne. How do we remember him today? As the person who started the Chundawat clan. It is that clan which has taken an oath to always protect

The Promised Crown

the Mewar throne yet never lay claim on it. Rawat Sangaji is his descendant and as fiercely loyal to the throne as his ancestors.'

Shakti sat up and held his mother's hand. 'I understand, ma. But I also see no future for me here. It will be either Pratap daada or Jagmal who will be the future king. Have you noticed how baapu gives me no expeditions to lead, no fights where I can show him that I am as good as daada?' he said, turning his face away. 'He doesn't think I am worthy.'

Sajja Bai's face fell. There was no denying that Udai Singh hadn't been fair. In spite of Pratap being constantly on expeditions, the Maharana had not given her son an opportunity to move out on the field.

'Ma,' Shakti said. 'I don't know whether others will understand me but I hope you do—whatever decision I come to.' With that he took her blessings and moved out of her chamber.

Meanwhile, out on the field, Pratap was engaged in yet another monologue with his stallion. 'We have moved around quite a bit in the last year, Chetak. Do you wish to go home? We have one more place to go to after which you can return to your wonderful thatched roof of Bassi. What do you say to that?'

The Promised Crown

It had been months since Pratap had taken off on an independent expedition to Vagarh. After his victory there, he had been packed off to handle several more. There was an assignment in Salumber and then Bali in the Marwar region. Finally, all three had been brought under Mewar's regime. En route, he had received a special message about Shakti Singh.

Pratap,

Please be warned that your brother Shakti now no longer belongs to us, Sisodias. We have received news that he has joined Akbar, the son of the Mughal, Humayun.

As Maharana, I have now exiled him from Mewar. At no point shall he return to this land. Beware, that if he tries to communicate with you, you shall meet the same fate.

In the present circumstances, your expeditions are of even greater value. We need to keep Mewar together.

Maharana Udai Singh

Pratap was furious at Shakti. His reading of his brother's character had been accurate. By joining this new Mughal king Akbar, he had brought about his own downfall. After all, hadn't Akbar's father, Humayun, been defeated by Sher Shah Suri who now ruled over the Dilli Sultanate?

'Yet, there is no underestimating the Mughals. I wonder what their next plan is?' Pratap shared his thoughts with Tej

Lal, the young soldier he had befriended over their many expeditions together. Tej was a soldier from the Bhil tribe. He reminded Pratap of Bhura and hence the prince was drawn to him.

Tej responded, 'We must never underestimate the power of the person who has been ignored, Kunwar.' Pratap knew what that meant. He had noticed how often Shakti felt sidelined at court or during their lessons together. He still remembered the look in Shakti's eyes the day he had defeated him in the face-off.

'This is a highly important decision, Maharanaji. It has been the tradition in not just Mewar but also other regimes—the key to building allies. Even the Mughals have started cementing marriage alliances with Hindu princesses to ensure supremacy and make inroads into Mewar,' Rawat Sanga told Udai Singh.

'Importantly, Kunwar Pratap and Rajkunwari Ajabde are familiar with each other. The Punwar family was here last year for the Gangaur festival,' added Rawat Kishandas.

Udai Singh pondered over this. Bringing Ajabde into the Sisodia family as Pratap's wife would definitely be an advantage for Mewar. Ajabde's father, Mamrakh Punwar, would be a strong ally during battle.

'Hmm, joint forces always work to an advantage. Let us send a messenger to Bijolia. Also, send a message to Pratap. Where is he currently?'

'Kunwar Pratap has set up camp at Mandalgarh and will leave in some days for home, Maharanaji. As you know, he has been very successful with the conquests against...'

'Yes, I am aware. Send him word to move towards Bijolia. By that time, the Punwars would have received my message. I expect him to accept immediately. The wedding will take place in Chittorgarh. Make the necessary arrangements. We will make the formal announcement as soon as we hear back from them,' said Udai Singh, moving back into his chamber.

Moments after he was gone, Rawat Sanga and Rawat Kishandas looked at each other.

'With all due respect, why does he not acknowledge Kunwar Pratap's accomplishments?' Rawat Sanga asked.

'We all know why, Rawatji. In the next ten years, Mewar will undergo a huge change. It will be very troublesome and some very tough decisions will need to be taken. These will test our loyalty to Mewar and to the Maharana. Will you be with me?' asked Rawat Kishandas.

Rawat Sanga nodded. 'Jai Mewar!'

Chittor's Final Celebration, c.1557

'Baapu's message has come once more, Chetak. Still no sight of home. We have to move towards Bijolia,' Pratap, as always, was busy talking to his companion, Chetak. 'We will pass by the Bhimlat temple and waterfall. Last year, when Patta, Rawat Sangaji's nephew, and Ajabde, Mamrakhji Punwar's daughter, came to Chittor for the Gangaur puja, Ajabde told us about the Bhimlat temple. She said the waterfall near the temple appears like milk flowing through the mountains. Patta was really young, barely five years old, but he wanted to ride on you and go there right away. Remember?'

'Chetak, enjoy your alone time with Kunwar Pratap. Your company will not be in demand soon,' a voice boomed from behind. Pratap zipped around to see Tej there.

Chittor's Final Celebration, c.1557

'That's one skill you need to teach me, Tej—sneaking up quietly!' smiled Pratap.

'Light-footedness gives me speed too, Kunwar. I'll teach you. For now, you have me to do the sneaking around for you,' said Tej. 'Aren't you interested to know about the new company you'll have soon?'

'In the field, I have all of you for company and my Chetak too. And, once in a while, along comes baapu's messenger. I can count all my company on my fingers. I assume you're talking about our return to Bassi. That's expected, once we finish this work in Bijolia. So, there's nothing to ask you!' quipped Pratap.

'Hmm. Usually I don't listen to news that floats about on the clouds, but this one I couldn't ignore. And if it's true, I'll be happy for you!' Tej grinned.

'Such puzzles! You really are just like Bhura. Someday you two must meet. Now out with whatever this floating-on-the-clouds news is—or go talk to the clouds!' responded Pratap with mock anger.

'It's about you and Rajkunwari Ajabde Punwar of Bijolia. A marriage proposal has been offered,' Tej replied in one go.

Pratap took a long time to respond. 'I knew this was coming, but I thought the purpose of this visit to Bijolia was different,' he said finally.

'You knew?' It was Tej's turn to be surprised.

'Last time when maiya visited, she spoke a lot about political alliances, as did Guru Avadhuta,' said Pratap. He smiled. 'Bijolia is close to the Malwa region. An alliance with the Punwars makes strategic sense. Importantly, I know Ajabde. She's highly intelligent and I really liked her understanding of Mewar and its administration. But Tej, most of the time, Rajkunwaris are not asked about their wish. I do hope Ajabde holds a good opinion about me, just as I do about her. What do you feel?'

'There's no doubt she does,' smiled Tej.

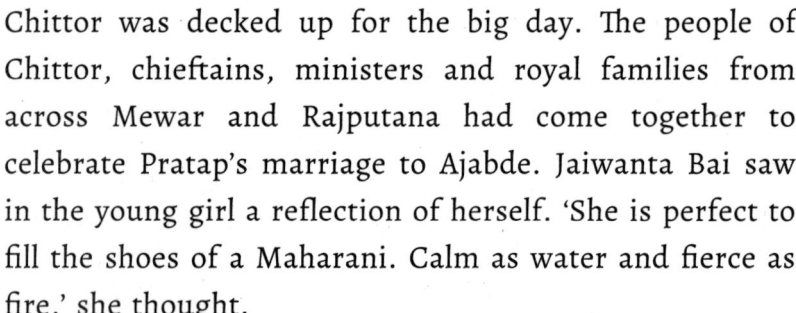

Chittor was decked up for the big day. The people of Chittor, chieftains, ministers and royal families from across Mewar and Rajputana had come together to celebrate Pratap's marriage to Ajabde. Jaiwanta Bai saw in the young girl a reflection of herself. 'She is perfect to fill the shoes of a Maharani. Calm as water and fierce as fire,' she thought.

While the city rejoiced, there was one person who was having sleepless nights. Dheer Bai was deeply concerned about Pratap's marriage. The eldest son would now have his own children, and the route for Jagmal to sit on the throne seemed fraught with multiple roadblocks.

Chittor's Final Celebration, c.1557

Sensing her thoughts, Udai Singh asked her, 'Dheer Bai, why do you worry so much all the time? Is little Jagmal tiring you out?'

'No, Maharanaji. Jagmal is the sweetest child ever born. He's only two but yesterday he was repeating Shree Eklingnathji's prayers with me. And that evening? Didn't you see him trying to pull your sword from its sheath? He seems naturally attracted to it!'

'I can see that you've been training him very well. He'll take after his great mother,' Udai Singh smiled indulgently.

'And his illustrious father, undoubtedly. But when I think about his future, I get terribly worried. He may receive all the praises, and is worthy of them, but he is among the last in a long line of brothers. I wonder what lies in store for my Jagmal!'

The Maharana sighed. 'We can't be going over this again, Dheer Bai. I've told you this earlier too. We have to wait for Jagmal to grow up to at least ten for me to understand his capabilities.'

'My words may have come out too strong, Maharanaji, please excuse me. But he is your son. And you are the most valiant and brave king I've ever seen—Mewar has ever seen! Stories of your valour are told to children to inspire them. Your unmatched strength and strategies will be spoken of for years to come,' she said, turning to him. 'And these are

hereditary gifts to Jagmal. I hope he isn't denied anything only because of the order of birth, Shree Eklingnathji!' Dheer Bai added dramatically.

'No one can deny him anything if Shree Eklingnathji Maharaj so wills.'

∼

Ajabde looked around. The Chittor palace and fort were huge, almost like a maze. But more than being fascinated by its beauty and grandeur, she was enthralled by the stories of valour of the women and men of Chittorgarh that she had heard since childhood. Her mother had told her how the women, led by Rani Padmini, and the men, led by Rawal Ratan Singh, had laid down their lives here.

'Honour before life, Ajabde. That has always been the Mewari rule,' she had said.

Ajabde's eyes welled up. She could almost hear the sounds of that raging battle of 1303, when Alauddin Khilji's forces had ravaged the fort. If that dark mark on its history wasn't enough, Chittor had seen another lethal attack more recently, before she was born. The Gujarat army led by Bahadur Shah had laid siege—and once again it was a battle to the finish for the Mewaris.

However, one particular story stood out in her memory, one that she liked to think of every night before bed—the

Chittor's Final Celebration, c.1557

story of a woman like no other. When all the women were headed towards jauhar, one of Maharana Sanga's queens had herself picked up the sword. She had opted for saka, just like the men.

'Are you thinking about your life in Bijolia, Ajabde?' Kunwar Pratap's voice interrupted her thoughts.

She smiled. 'Quite the contrary. I am thinking about life, as it has been, in Chittor. The walls of this fort, this palace, have so many stories to tell.'

'Stories, yes, several. I would like to rewrite some of them,' said Pratap, reminiscing, just like Ajabde, the various sieges Chittor had seen.

'We will pray to Shree Eklingnathji Maharaj. My maiya says his blessings give strength.'

Pratap nodded.

A thought suddenly came to Ajabde. 'Kunwarji, what do you think of women?'

'Women are strong, resilient, brave. They have an inherent understanding of politics and are adept at people management. They can nurture the future. They can be the future. They are the backbone of any family.'

Ajabde looked at him with great pride and love. She felt a deep sense of happiness at the thought of being his partner in life. She was aware that he too, as rulers did in this era, would go on to marry other princesses. But she

and Pratap shared something special. They were friends and their thoughts aligned on important matters.

'Ajabde? You do seem quite frightful with that lost look on your face! Come back to the present.' Pratap laughed.

Ajabde laughed back. She was annoyed with him but that was an apt description of how she might have looked. 'I was thinking about how you were as a child,' she replied, quickly thinking of a way to wriggle out of the situation.

'Right! I believe you!' responded Pratap.

When their banter ended, they sat quietly, watching the sunset.

'Maiya told me that story about Rani Jawahir Bai,' Ajabde said, turning towards Pratap. 'That instead of committing jauhar, she took up the sword and fought Bahadur Shah's army!'

'I have heard it too,' replied Pratap. 'It fills me with pride that she decided to do that.'

'I wonder if history would have been written differently if all the women had followed what she did?' Ajabde asked hesitantly, unsure of what Pratap would say.

Pratap pondered the question. 'When I say I am proud that Rani Jawahir Bai picked up the sword, it doesn't mean I'm not proud of what Rani Padmini and Rani Karnavati did. These decisions were taken because we Mewaris live by the principle of honour before life.'

Chittor's Final Celebration, c.1557

Ajabde nodded, remembering what her mother had told her.

'But I understand what you are asking too. The answer to that lies in education. I think we educate our boys and girls differently. If both are taught to fight, then during a battle, the women too can come to the field. If both are taught resource management, then the men too can handle resources efficiently. One way or the other, they have to manage the fort—outside and within.'

'But those who manage things within are never celebrated, are they?' Ajabde looked at Pratap.

The Rise of Jalal

'HE IS NOT YET SIXTEEN BUT IS KNOWN TO BE AS FIERCE AS his grandfather Babur, Maharanaji.' Bharmal Kawadia had gathered all the information on the rising new power in the Mughal empire—Akbar. 'He is still under the guardianship of Bairam Khan, his father Humayun's loyal general. Those who have seen him fight against the Afghans in Kalanaur say that he has the skill and ruthlessness of the Mughals etched in his very being.'

Rawat Sanga, Rawat Kishandas, Bharmal Kawadia and Udai Singh were discussing the grave new developments in the region. Ever since his father's death and his subsequent coronation, Akbar was being spoken of with great trepidation in every court that had seen Mughal invasion in the past.

The Maharanas of Mewar were no exception. They had been in direct conflict with the Mughals. Udai Singh's thoughts raced back to history. In the Battle of Khanua in

The Rise of Jalal

1527, Maharana Sanga had led a coalition of Rajputs and non-Rajputs against Babur. He carried the reputation of being undefeatable. On the other hand, Babur had just won the First Battle of Panipat against Ibrahim Lodi of the Dilli Sultanate—a battle that had established the Mughal presence in India. He had won decisively in Khanua too, a victory that eventually led to Maharana Sanga's death and the dramatic events that followed in the Sisodia clan. Udai Singh remembered the dark days when his own uncle Banveer had wanted to kill him, and how his Panna Dai had sacrificed her son's life for his protection.

'Just like his grandfather, Akbar too is riding on his big win against Hemu of the Afghan Sur dynasty of Dilli. Coincidentally, this battle also played out at Panipat,' added Bharmal. 'He has only one mission—to expand the Mughal Sultanate. He has recently taken over Mewat and Alwar, very close to us. But according to my spies, he has moved towards the north now. It is the Jammu region that he is eyeing.'

Udai Singh took his time to assess the situation. 'Hmm. His father did not carry his grandfather's reputation, so it looks like we have underestimated this young boy. We will have to monitor his movements very closely. If the Mughals are gaining strength again, we had better be prepared. Let us make arrangements to move to Udaipur soon. The less known about our whereabouts, the better.'

Then, he hesitantly asked, 'Where is Shakti? Any news of his whereabouts after Chittor?'

Rawat Sanga, who had kept a keen eye on the Maharana's exiled son, replied, 'Maharanaji, he went to Akbar's court but has not been able to impress him much. We suspect that Akbar feels that Mewari loyalty still exists in him. Hence Kunwar Shakti has not been able to secure any favours from him yet.'

'Do not call him Kunwar any longer, Rawat Sangaji!' Udai Singh's voice quivered with anger. 'Some don't deserve that respect. Which region has Pratap been assigned to now?'

'You have assigned him to Dariba, Maharanaji. He is taking steps to fortify the mines there. The Zawar, Agucha and Dariba mines have been attracting invaders too. From what I have learnt, most of the work in Dariba is completed and he will move with the contingent to Zawar,' said Rawat Kishandas.

'Keep him notified of these new developments on the Mughal front. Pratap will know how to speed up the matter.' Dark times seemed to lie ahead for Mewar. Udai Singh would have to stand tall.

∽

'Lakhiji Meena, how long do you think it will take us to secure the area?' Tej Lal asked the chieftain's son as Kunwar Pratap assessed the mines of Zawar.

Lakhi had not warmed up to the sudden arrival of the prince of Mewar with his contingent. He was especially wary of Tej Lal, who seemed very close to the Kunwar and quite adamant too.

In response to the question, he turned to Pratap and smiled. 'Kunwarji, Zawar is different from Dariba. Since Dariba is in the maidaani area, it needs more fortifying. But we, at Zawar? We are in the pahadi area, naturally protected by the hills and thick forests. We have been blessed by Zawarmata.'

'I know you have been blessed,' Pratap said, smiling back. 'Yet, if we wish to stay independent, we need to keep our guard up, Lakhiji.'

Tej Lal had taken offence to Lakhi ignoring him. He did a quick estimation and said, 'It should take us a month to go around the mines, Kunwarji. We can have a barricade of rocks and that would protect the mines very well.'

Pratap sensed the animosity between the two—something he didn't want to encourage. He knew that if he had to protect this highly valuable yet vulnerable area, he would need the cooperation of the Meena Bhils.

'Right said, Tej. But that's not your way, is it, Lakhiji?' he said, signalling Tej to calm down and turning towards the chieftain's son.

Lakhi looked at his prince and smiled. 'Kunwarji, you know us very well! We work with bows-arrows and boulders.

We work in stealth mode. With all due respect, protection is important to us, but in our style.'

'You're right. Not only do I understand your ways well but I also have huge respect for them. Most of my warfare tactics have been taught to me by my friends from the Bhil community. But do give a thought to my suggestion. The invaders—they don't come with bows and arrows, sometimes not even with swords. They come with gunpowder and large cannons. Their style of warfare is new and very different from ours. Which is why I emphasise the need to stand together. But the most important thing is that I'd like to work with you, not against your wishes,' said Pratap.

Allowing Lakhi to mull over his words, he then asked him, 'Could I meanwhile get some kodo ki roti or maybe mawa kachoris? I would be delighted. It's been a long way from Dariba and I am very hungry. My friend Bhura's maiya back in the jungles of Kumbhalgarh used to make these for me.'

Lakhi was visibly surprised. 'Aren't you eating with your men, Kunwarji?' No prince of Mewar had shared meals with them.

'If you don't mind, I'd really like to eat in your company. But if there's a problem, we can manage our food arrangements by ourselves,' replied Pratap.

'Oh no! We'd be honoured,' said Lakhi immediately.

The Rise of Jalal

By night, over a hearty meal, the Meena Bhils had come to an understanding with Pratap.

And, by the end of the month, Pratap had not only got the area barricaded but also won the hearts of the Meena Bhils. Moreover, he had formed a close friendship with Lakhi.

'Kunwarji, I pray that Zawarmata always takes care of you and of Mewar. However, it is Lakhi's promise to you that he and his men will be there for you, if you ever need them.'

I Am the Ruler

Akbar stood at a *jharokha* at the Gagron fort. He looked out at the expanse of water and land ahead. The Kali Sindh and Ahu rivers conjoined here, covering the fort from three sides, while the fourth side was all rocky terrain. The *jala durg* had seen countless battles, including several sakas and jauhars that the people of the land prided themselves on. The stories of the past didn't fascinate him. For Akbar, the fort and its surrounding area held supreme importance because it would serve as his second pair of eyes on Mewar—a land that seemed to resist Mughal influence with tenacity.

Ajmer was his first post close to Mewar. He had set up his headquarters there after defeating Rao Maldeo Rathore of Jodhpur and annexing the triangle of Ajmer, Nagaur and Jetaran. Together, these would help him gain a stranglehold on Mewar.

I Am the Ruler

Mewar—he was enamoured by the place. It had minacious plains, dramatic mountains, and rivers that in spate could both protect and destroy.

'Baba,' Akbar finally spoke to his guardian, Bairam Khan, who stood beside him, 'we must set up headquarters here. It will help us move into Mewar, into Chittor, and force Udai Singh into submission. It will...'

Bairam frowned. He thought the idea was overambitious. 'Jalal, Jalal! We've only just set up base in Ajmer. If you spread yourself thin, you will never grow to be the...'

'Baba, I do think I'm old enough to think for myself,' Akbar interrupted, his tone sharp.

Bairam Khan didn't want to agitate the young ruler further and tried to pacify him. Of late, anything he said or did seemed to annoy Akbar. 'Of course, you're old enough, Jalal. Not just old enough, you are an intelligent and smart ruler. I only meant to speak in favour of the Mughal empire...'

'I didn't finish, baba. I am old enough to think for myself *and* my empire,' Akbar replied icily.

'Time for baba to go! Time for baba to go!' Akbar's Hiramani parrot spoke up at that very moment. Hiramani parrots were a speciality of Gagron. They were larger than others of their kind and had completely red heads with spotted bodies. But what made them special—and much sought after—was that they could speak in a human voice. When Akbar had taken over Gagron, a trader from Malwa

I Am the Ruler

had come to pay his respects and gifted him 'Hira', as Akbar lovingly called the bird.

'Baba, did you hear Hira? Time for you to go,' said Akbar, playfully tapping the bird's head with his finger.

Bairam Khan was furious. However, he bit his tongue. The boy had turned eighteen and was now the supreme ruler of the Mughal dynasty. He was gaining power in Hindustan, and it was in Bairam's best interest to stay aligned with him.

'*Hukum*,' he said and retreated.

'And, baba, arrange to have Gagron made my headquarters.'

'Yes, yes, of course.'

'You did well to send off Bairam Khan to Mecca, Jalal. He has lived his life and he'd better be thinking about Allah now instead of meddling in the empire's affairs,' said Maham Anga. 'Your plan to make Gagron our second headquarters is apt. It will give us a grip over the south-east of Mewar, and we can close in on our prize—Chittor, and then all of Mewar. I will send for Adham immediately and he can draw up a plan for the same.'

Akbar smiled as Maham Anga spoke. He had the utmost respect for her. She had taken care of him as a baby and guided him through the most tumultuous years since his

father's death. But, of late, her overenthusiasm in decision-making and her growing interference exasperated him. And then there was her younger son, Adham Khan, who was increasingly becoming a source of concern. He definitely needed to be reined in.

'Maham Ammi, Adham has done well in helping us conquer Gagron, but I have decided that Shams-ud-Din Ataga Khan will be in charge here. He is loyal and has a deep understanding of political and administrative nuances.'

Maham Anga hesitated. She couldn't let her face betray any hint of disappointment. 'Of course! Ataga Khan is very skilful and his loyalty is beyond question. Would you like Adham to help you with any new expeditions then? As you acknowledged, he is a great fighter and will win you many a battle! He is your foster brother after all,' she said, smiling.

Akbar stared out of the *jharokha* again. 'It really looks beautiful from here, doesn't it?' he said, turning to Maham Anga. 'I would rather he go hunting, Maham Ammi,' he added, before she could respond.

Maham Anga was taken aback but remained expressionless.

'It is beautiful indeed. You're right. You always take such good care of your brother. He has been working constantly for the last few months, and the break will do him good. I will inform him.'

'Foster, Maham Ammi,' said Akbar, as Maham Anga turned to move out.

'Excuse me, Jalal, I didn't hear you...' she replied, looking rather quizzically at Akbar.

'Adham is my foster brother,' he smiled and turned back to his viewing spot.

'Ammi, he is getting too big for his boots! Just control him or else he will have to bear the strength of my sword,' Adham Khan raged in the safety of his chamber. Only his mother was present in the room.

'Quiet, Adham. Sometimes, I really wish Allah would give you some brains along with that enormous body of yours!' Maham Anga scolded her son.

'Ammi!' he shouted back.

'Keep your voice low, son. If Jalal or any of his loyal men hear you, there will be no escape from his wrath. Not even your ammi will be able to intervene. Do you understand?'

Stomping the floor, Adham Khan slumped into his chair.

'Look at me. I'm as frustrated as you with the way things are at court. But do I let it reflect on my face? No. Because I mask my emotions well—unlike you, who is being an utter fool. I'm sure your exploits have reached Jalal's ears, else he

wouldn't have turned down my suggestion of giving you the responsibility of Gagron. He has selected that pest, Ataga Khan!' she thundered. 'If only I hadn't chosen Ataga's wife to feed Jalal as an infant! He holds the family very close to his heart.'

'I will kill Ataga, Ammi. Yes, that's what I'll do,' murmured Adham, fire in his eyes.

'Hussssh! Are you absolutely out of your mind, Adham? Stay within your limits. We will get our chances.'

Friendship with Benefits, c.1565

'I DON'T AGREE WITH THE USE OF ONLY MUSCLE POWER. IN the present circumstances, we must have a Rajput policy. Strategise before you act,' said Akbar.

He had just broken free of the shackles of his foster mother, Maham Anga, and his foster brother, Adham Khan. *A little too savagely perhaps, but Adham Khan had asked for it,* thought Akbar. *How dare he kill Ataga Khan?* Adham deserved to be thrown off that ledge. It was unfortunate that Maham Ammi couldn't bear the loss. *Would she have approved of my Rajput policy? Most definitely not.* In a way, Akbar was glad to be free of that suffocating stranglehold.

His thoughts returned to the present. His independent council of ministers sat before him. The very young Man Singh was seated to his left. He was the son of Bhagwant

Das, the ruler of Amber. Akbar sought his counsel, as he knew Mewar very well and, as a young prince, often came up with unique ideas.

'What do you say Kunwar Man Singh?'

'Different people, different approaches, *Jahaanpanah*, I would say,' replied Man Singh.

As a Rajput, it was unlikely he would ever forget the time when Amber came under Mughal rule. In fact, it was among the first to bow down to Akbar. Man Singh's grandfather, Bharmal, had met the young Mughal about five or six years ago and paid his respects. Then, in 1562, he had given Harka Bai, his daughter and Man Singh's aunt, in marriage to Akbar.

'You mean to say there are kings who would not respect a marriage alliance with me?' asked Akbar, amused.

Man Singh knew what had tickled him. Akbar was a powerful man, with the wealth and military might to conquer almost any region. The thought that someone might refuse a matrimonial alliance with him must have seemed laughable.

Man Singh cleared his throat and said, 'I sense that Bikaner and Jesalmer might be won over, but some others won't. Definitely not Mewar,' he added, meeting the emperor's gaze.

'I like that you never hesitate to give me a precise understanding of the situation, Kunwar Man Singh. You're

Friendship with Benefits, c.1565

never afraid to speak up. Most people are,' Akbar smiled. But he couldn't digest Mewar's stubbornness.

'Why is Mewar so? Why would they not like my rule? Do they think I won't be a just ruler? Do they feel I'm not accepting of their religions and cultures? What is it?' he asked, deeply disappointed.

'With due respect, *Jahaanpanah*,' Man Singh replied, 'it doesn't matter who you are or what you do or don't—the Mewari rulers are known across the lands for their valour, strength and the premium they place on self-respect. They are fiercely independent and will never succumb to an invader.'

'Mind your words, Kunwar Man! It's the Mughal empire you're speaking of, not some lowly invaders!' Akbar thundered.

But the young Man Singh was not easily disturbed. 'Excuse me, *Jahaanpanah*. I didn't mean to offend. I was building up to the idea of the Rajput policy you've suggested. You will have to customise it wherever you go. We call it *saam, daam, dand, bhed*. That means you either persuade or buy out, punish or divide to achieve your goal.'

'*Aatmasammanah praadhanyam*. It means self-respect is our priority. Do you agree, Rawat Patta?' Pratap asked the young boy sitting with him.

'Daada, please don't call me Rawat Patta. It makes me feel so old. I'm only fourteen, you know!' Patta protested.

Pratap laughed and joined his hands in reverence. 'Well, you'd better get used to being called so. You represent the great Chundawat clan, Rawat Pattaji, and we Sisodias are always indebted to you for your support and protection. Moreover, when I was as young as you, my *Guruji* always called me Kunwar Pratap. We are born into this. There is no escape.'

'It's not about escaping; it just feels very odd when it comes from you. I've always taken you to be my older brother,' smiled Patta.

Just then, Patta's uncle, Rawat Sanga, walked towards them.

'Jai Shree Eklingnathji Maharaj, Rawatji. I'm very pleased you brought Rawat Pattaji along,' said Pratap, mischievously grinning at his young friend, who rolled his eyes.

'It has been a long year of expeditions around the Aravallis and I was looking forward to meeting all of you. Rawat Pattaji makes me look forward to Amar's teenage years.'

'Jai Shree Eklingnathji Maharaj, Kunwar Pratap. Patta always speaks of you, and when we heard of your return, we came along to meet you,' replied Rawat Sanga. 'I have just met Kunwar Amar. Just as with your weaponry education,

Friendship with Benefits, c.1565

Maharanaji has asked me to oversee his. That child is very skilful—just like his father,' he added, smiling at Pratap.

'I will address Amar as Kunwar Amar Singhji henceforth,' announced Patta suddenly, looking quite delighted with the idea.

'Patta, it would help to speak a bit more maturely. You're speaking to Kunwar Pratap!' Rawat Sanga admonished his nephew.

'No, no, Rawatji. Patta is my younger brother. If he won't tease me, I'll start to feel very old!' Pratap smiled, sending Patta off.

'I'd like to know one thing though,' he said, lowering his voice. 'My people have informed me that Akbar has set his eyes on Mewar. Elaborate plans are being drawn, food supplies are being ramped up and new soldiers recruited and trained, I'm told. What does your spy network say?'

Rawat Sanga was hardly surprised that Pratap had his own network of spies. In fact, he was proud that he did. It helped to have your ears on the street.

'The situation is serious, Kunwar. Maharanaji has been made aware of what's going on. He will soon call you and the council to discuss this. Let's be prepared.'

'But why is this Akbar so interested in Mewar, Daada?' asked Patta, when he and Pratap were alone later.

'The lure of power, Patta, is great. So great that one is blind to everything else,' replied Pratap, deep in thought. 'But Mewar is special to Akbar and his Mughal dynasty because we fall in the line of his trade, which is one of the ways he makes money. That money eventually gives him the power to expand further. Whether he wants to trade with Gujarat or with the Deccan, he needs to pass through our land.'

'So, he needs friends, not enemies,' suggested Patta.

'But I don't like his style of friendship,' said Pratap sharply. 'And his subjugation—we won't agree to. So, you see, my friend, we are poised for great enmity.'

'*Aatmasammanah praadhanyam*, Daada.'

The Fall, 1567-1571

'No, Baapu. This is not how we must handle Akbar.' It was the first time anyone had heard Pratap openly oppose his father.

'Even if it were the very last battle of our life, we must stand together and fight,' he said, looking straight at the Maharana. His gaze was unwavering.

Udai Singh shook his head in exasperation. 'Pratap, I understand your emotions are running high, but have you properly heard what Shakti has just told us? Akbar's army is marching towards Chittor. Akbar himself told him this. In fact, he invited him to join. Shakti has been offered a lucrative reward by that invader—the throne of Mewar!"

He looked at Shakti, strangely surprised and proud that the son he had exiled chose not to take the offer. Instead, Shakti returned to Chittor to warn them of the danger looming ahead.!'

Then he turned towards Pratap, who was in no mood to be persuaded.

'We, Pratap, are outnumbered. And not just that—we do not possess the weapons they have. They use gunpowder to overpower armies,' he thundered.

The court went silent.

Pratap looked at his brother, Shakti, who had returned after years, only to become the harbinger of doom. Yet he was proud of what his brother had done. Shakti had shown the mettle a Mewari ought to possess—to bury past differences with his family and warn them of a direct and elaborate attack.

Shakti spoke, turning to his brother.

'Daada, please don't think of staying back and defending Chittor. I've spent a considerable amount of time with him.'

Pratap looked sharply at him, and Shakti hesitated before continuing.

'P-pardon me, but I do know how he thinks. I know his army's strength. We don't stand a chance.'

This time, the silence ran deep.

Udai Singh broke it. 'I am the Maharana. I must take a broader perspective of things.'

'And that perspective involves us leaving for Udaipur and letting our generals face the barbaric Akbar as he barges into Chittorgarh?' Pratap replied, bracing himself. He was simmering with rage.

'Maharanaji, if I may?'

Guru Avadhuta spoke up. The Maharana nodded.

Pratap didn't need his father to respond now—nor the king of the land.

'Kunwar Pratap, we've often debated short-term gains and long-term wins, haven't we? All of us here agree that staying back in Chittor will not help Mewar in the long run. It is imperative that the Maharana and his family be protected in the face of imminent danger,' he explained.

'But what of the *dharma* of a ruler?' Pratap asked at once.

'When there is no ruler, what *dharma* are we speaking of? It is important that the ruler lives, so that *dharma* can be upheld at a later time,' replied Guru Avadhuta calmly.

'If the future turns to me and debates my decision, the responsibility will be mine and mine alone,' Udai Singh declared.

'At least I can be here, Baapu,' Pratap pleaded.

But that was not to be.

In 1567, Udai Singh left with his family and the royal treasury for Udaipur. Left to guard the grand Chittorgarh were a young Rawat Patta and the chieftain of Merta, Jaimal Rathor.

The Fall, 1567-1571

It had been four months since Akbar laid siege to Chittorgarh, and tonight seemed to be the final night.

Rawat Patta sat in silence with his mother, Sajjan Bai of Songara, and his wife, Phool Kanwar of Merta. The chief caretaker of the fort, Jaimal Rathor, had just fallen to a gunshot from Akbar. Outside, the battle raged. The enemy was inching closer to the inner sanctum. The inevitable stared them in the face.

It was Patta's responsibility now.

'*Mai*, let's face the jauhar and saka with pride on our faces,' he said, with as much bravery as an eighteen-year-old could muster.

'No. *Mai*, let's all face the saka with pride,' Phool Kanwar spoke up.

'W-what do you mean, Phool?' Patta said, his voice quivering.

His mother drew a long breath. 'She means that those women who can must shed their blood for Mewar. If they are to give up their lives, they must take up the sword!'

Patta was aghast, but his mother and wife wasted no time. They donned the *kesariya* robes and picked up swords. All three then screamed out, 'Jai Mewar!' and charged at the incoming troops.

~

The fall of Chittorgarh shook Udai Singh. It was violent. It was brutal. It was barbaric. The siege had lasted four months. In the end, not a single soldier stood.

Multiple jauhars were held in the fort, charring the aged, the women and the children to death. Countless women died in battle. But the worst part? Akbar had walked into the fort and ordered the killing of all innocent civilians who had taken shelter within its walls.

In spite of Chittorgarh's fall, Udai Singh still ruled over much of Mewar—especially the mountainous regions. He had taken off to Udaipur, then to Kumbhalgarh, and thereafter to Gogunda, making it his capital. The Mughal army pursued him for months, but in vain. To their surprise, they were no match for the speed and skill of the Mewari soldiers. Additionally, the Mewaris had the advantage of knowing every inch of the terrain.

To compensate for this disadvantage, wherever the Mughal soldiers went looking for the Maharana, they ravaged the land. It was a sorry tale.

Udai Singh was a tired man now. Not so much because of age, but because of the emotional devastation that came with the fall of Chittor.

'I don't believe this. Has Akbar truly defeated the ruler of Ranthambore and taken over Ranthambore?' he asked, genuinely surprised, as Pratap brought him the news. His son nodded. The Maharana drew a long breath.

The Fall, 1567–1571

'Pratap, I don't know if your maiya has ever told you—in my childhood, I kept moving from place to place to escape my uncle Banveer. My Panna Dai placed her own son on my bed, leaving him to die, while she smuggled me out of the palace to safety.' He paused. Pratap held his hand.

'Am I at the end of the road now, Pratap? Life seems to have come full circle. I'm again moving from place to place,' Udai Singh let out a sad laugh.

For the first time, Pratap saw his father look older than he was.

'I chose to move away from the bloodbath at Chittorgarh. But how am I ever to escape my restless nights? They are filled with the endless screams of men, women, the aged and the children. You told me, Pratap—I remember well—that you told me to stay. To fight. To give up my life, if it came to that. I thought I knew better,' he said, continuing his monologue.

Pratap was far from comforted. He was disappointed with the decision and heartbroken by the outcome. Even four years after that dreadful siege, he continued to fight his own demons. Like his father, he had not had a moment's rest.

The news of Patta and his family's death had hit him the hardest. His blood boiled every time he heard of yet another Mughal conquest—and there were many.

Rawat Sanga had stood like a lion, undefeated in spirit, through it all. Whenever Pratap looked at him, a sense of purpose surged through him.

For now, it was time to lie low, yet keep strengthening the military and rebuilding the royal treasury. He held on to his father's hand. Pratap knew that this was not the last time Akbar had trained his guns on Mewar.

Destiny of a Maharana, c.1572

'What do you think, Ajabde? Is my decision flawed? Will history mock me for doing what I am about to do?'

His father had died and a new drama had unfolded in the palace—or was about to unfold. Pratap had come straight to the person he felt would take a neutral view of the situation. He was certain that only Ajabde could think through this. He was emotionally disturbed, and his mother seemed to be in the same state of mind. He didn't want to put her through the dilemma of choosing between her husband, who now lay dead, and her son.

For Ajabde too, it was a rather delicate situation. The unthinkable had happened. Her father-in-law, the Maharana, had willed the throne of Mewar to his much younger and inexperienced son, Jagmal, on the persuasion of Dheer Bai.

What was a mere rumour in the corridors of the palace had turned into a fact. In no time, it would be known to every person in Mewar and beyond. There could be new armies marching up to the gates to fight the inexperienced king. On the other hand, Pratap had decided to leave Mewar forever to avoid conflict with his brother and any civil outrage.

She finally spoke. 'What is done is done, Kunwarji. We need to face the present. I have just one thought. Why don't you continue to stay in Gogunda? It is a bitter question, but answering it will help you get some clarity. Is the thought of staying under the subjugation of your younger brother bothering you, or is it something else? Spell it out.'

Pratap drew a long breath. 'I love Mewar, Ajabde. I have a vision for my kingdom. I don't want it to be wasted by invaders like Akbar. I have the will and the courage to fight him and anyone else who raises their head against Mewar. If I see Jagmal not doing that, I will be extremely upset. Imagine having the power to fight a situation but having your hands tied. Staying here will feel like that.'

Ajabde nodded.

'Also, I don't know how people will react to this news. If they don't see me every day, they may make their peace with Jagmal, whatever they feel about him,' concluded Pratap.

Ajabde placed her hand on his shoulder, looked into his eyes and said, 'But will it be right? A ruler needs to assess

Destiny of a Maharana, c.1572

that. Mewar needs you. And once a ruler knows that his land needs him, he must make every effort to stay in power.'

Pratap looked at her. Many years ago, Guru Avadhuta had said those very words.

The Gogunda palace had been readying for Holi the next day when the news of the Maharana's passing came. Given the financial constraints of the family after the siege of Chittorgarh, the celebrations would have been subdued. But this news put everything on hold and the state was in mourning.

Rawat Sanga, Rawat Kishandas and Bharmal Kawadia had arranged for the last rites. The queens present in Gogunda—Jaiwanta Bai and Dheer Bai—stood close by. The children of the Maharana were in attendance. The council of the Maharana was there. Pratap was absent though.

'Guru Avadhuta has informed Pratap that, as the successor to the throne, he must not be present at the funeral,' said Bharmal Kawadia, acknowledging this absence. But it was Rawat Kishandas who scanned the gathering and noticed that even Jagmal was missing. 'Why is Kunwar Jagmal not present at his father's funeral?' he whispered to the other two. 'This can mean only one thing!'

The trio swiftly moved to the court of the deceased Maharana where, as expected, Jagmal had claimed the throne.

'Kunwar Jagmal! I ask as the prime minister of Mewar—why are you on the throne?' demanded Bharmal Kawadia angrily. 'That throne carries the legacy of Mewar and only the rightful heir must occupy it. And that is Kunwar Pratap.'

'Kunwar Pratap indeed!' scoffed Jagmal. 'And who dares defy Maharana Udai Singh's will? You, Prime Minister Bharmalji? You may check with any of those present—Guru Avadhutaji, Rajvaidya Dhanurtiji, or my *ma*. I,' he announced dramatically, 'am the heir to the throne. By the Maharana's wish.'

By this time, Rawat Sanga and Rawat Kishandas had sprung into action. If Jagmal was on the throne by the Maharana's will, then Pratap must be preparing to leave Mewar.

∼

They were not wrong. Ajabde's advice was sound, but Pratap was hurt beyond measure. He had probably thought that he had earned his father's blessings, but this turn of events made him question everything—his baapu, his vision for Mewar, even the meaning of being born into the Sisodia clan. Disillusioned, he was readying Chetak to leave Gogunda.

Destiny of a Maharana, c.1572

'Where do you think you're going, Keeka?' a familiar voice called out. Pratap turned to find his childhood friend Bhura standing there.

Bhura embraced him and condoled his father's death. 'I am sure the Maharana is content in his resting place, Keeka. He knows he has left Mewar in safe hands,' he said, holding his friend by the shoulders. Pratap averted his eyes. He placed the saddle on Chetak.

'Or hasn't he?' Bhura asked, sensing something amiss.

Ajabde knew there wasn't much she could do. Besides, she had to be present for the funeral, so she made her way there. She knew how independent her husband was. In spite of what she had said, he had decided to leave Gogunda. She had no options left now, except maybe sounding off his mother.

She discreetly let Jaiwanta Bai know about the happenings, but the queen did not so much as bat an eyelid. From Dheer Bai's demeanour, she had already understood that the deed had been deviously planned and executed. As the eldest queen, she couldn't leave the gathering, but she had observed the swiftness with which Bharmal Kawadia, Rawat Sanga and Rawat Kishandas had left. She was sure they would take things under control.

Rawat Sanga and Rawat Kishandas, along with a few other nobles, came galloping towards Pratap. They were much relieved to see that Bhura was with him and had kept him engaged.

'One fights against the wrong; one doesn't succumb to it. Who better than you to know and understand that, Kunwar Pratap?' Rawat Sanga said, shaking him out of his stupor.

'The time has come to choose between your duty as a son and duty as a ruler, Keeka. You cannot go wrong today.'

Meanwhile, Rawat Kishandas had identified a rock nearby that could serve as a temporary throne for the new ruler.

And thus it happened—the *rajtilak* of one of the most valorous kings Mewar was to see. It was soon to be dusk and nobody wanted to risk wasting any more time. A few nobles and a dear friend were in attendance. Pratap sat on a rock at the entry of the Gogunda fort, and the air was filled with chants of '*Maharana Pratap ki jai!*' It was Holi in Mewar.

At the court, Jagmal had been throwing tantrums. Unfortunately, he had to be physically picked up from the throne and made to sit among the council. Greatly annoyed, he stomped out. Not just from the court, but also from Mewar.

The Resistance

'Keeka, the defeat of this man is possible. We must not plan this as a full head-on fight. He can only be weakened and brought to his knees by dhad. We will need to train our soldiers and generals in techniques that Akbar has not tasted yet,' Bhura told Pratap.

Pratap nodded. It was true. His army, his weaponry, his coffers—nothing was a match for Akbar's. The men were outnumbered two to one. The treasury was only dwindling due to constant attacks. Akbar had gunpowder. Dhad, the Bhils' style of guerrilla warfare, could be their key to retaliation, safety and independence.

Neither had the crown of Mewar come easy to Pratap nor did life look comfortable as its ruler. But Pratap knew better than to complain. Unlike the rest of India, Mewar was still a thorn in Akbar's flesh. Without Mewar, Akbar didn't have full control over the commercial routes to Gujarat or

the Deccan—and that was putting a strain on the empire's income.

On the other hand, Pratap knew he wasn't having it easy either. Once a sizeable independent region, Mewar was now largely controlled by the Mughals—directly or through their appointed caretakers. Most of the northern, eastern and western territories had been usurped by Akbar.

Pratap ran his finger across the map in front of him. The green flag, bearing a half sun and a lion, fluttered across the region. The Mughals' intention was clear—to isolate Mewar from the rest of India and, finally, force Pratap into submission.

'From Kamrup in the east to Ahmedabad in the west, and from Kashmir up north to Gwalior and Khandesh here—that's where he rules. Among Rajputs, he has power over the Bhatis of Jesalmer, the Kachhwahas of Jaipur, and the Hadas of Bundi,' Bhamashah elaborated. He was as sharp as his father, Bharmal Kawadia, who had served as prime minister to Udai Singh.

'Interestingly, he doesn't threaten the kings or their independence openly. He proposes marriage alliances with the royal family—either for himself or his kin. He grants *jagirs*, positions in court, and generous rewards to their relatives. In return, all he wants is revenue, allegiance to the Mughal empire, and a contingent in times of war,' Rawat Kishandas added.

'Soon, Rawat Kishandasji, they will not be allowed to hold independent views on foreign matters. After that, Akbar will interfere in coronations, and eventually in succession too. They'll become so dependent on him that their very identity will be wiped out. It's a strategic and long-term move to consolidate power over his—what does he call them—*mansabs*,' Pratap said. 'He's not doing this only for himself, I'll give him that. History will glorify him as the man who built an empire,' he added, pointing at the map. 'But his true goal is to secure the future of the Mughal dynasty. He's deeply affected by what happened to his father. He's doing this for his lineage—just like we do.'

'Maharanaji, then we too must cement our place in history. We need to strategise. Akbar is breaking up the land and ruling the pieces. We need to fit the pieces back together. That will come as a bolt from the blue for Akbar,' Rawat Sanga said. The bitterness of losing his young nephew at Chittorgarh echoed in his voice. 'We may have lost the battle—but we will not lose the war.'

~

'I am leaving you in charge, Ajabde, and I am sure you will be in complete control of things,' Pratap said. Before she could respond, it was Amar Singh who jumped in with a loud, 'Yes!'

The Resistance

'Now you're Ajabde, is it? Your baapu is talking to your ma. I will be in control when he isn't here—not you, young Kunwar,' she smiled, pulling up the young prince.

Pratap ruffled his son's hair. Then he turned to his wife again. 'There's something else I need to have your consent on, Ajabde.'

She sat beside him.

'I see very challenging times ahead. To beat this man, we can't stay in the lap of luxury. Sooner or later, we will have to leave the safety of our forts and the comfort of our palaces—and live in the lap of mother nature. No cosy beds or soft blankets. Meals will be simple—sometimes even absent.'

'The luxury of independence—will he still have that?' Ajabde asked. 'If yes, I am with you, Maharanaji. And I will train everyone in the household to prepare for what lies ahead.'

'Shree Eklingnathji Maharaj has blessed me with the best. Someone who is unshakeable in the toughest of times,' Pratap said, smiling at her. 'But how can the royal family be trained for this?'

'All of us will give up sleeping on beds starting today. We will forgo lavish meals and stop eating in gold and silverware. Special dishes will be made only once in two months. The rule will be binding on one and all in the palace,' she declared. 'These hardships are trivial. They will pass. But there's something else that troubles me, Maharanaji.'

Pratap looked at her.

'It pains me that we are destroying our own crops and fields. We are asking our farmers to till hilly regions with tools that don't suit that terrain. I wonder how we will cope. Maharanaji, it's not war that sustains a kingdom—it is food.'

Pratap had to agree. It wasn't something he was proud of either. But there was no other way. If the invading troops had access to food, they would never tire or retreat.

'This scorched earth policy is tearing me apart too, Ajabde. It troubles me to burn standing crops, to fill wells with debris, and to drive our farmers into the hills. Had there been another way, I would have taken it. But I have a plan—and with Shree Eklingnathji Maharaj's blessings, I'll be able to execute it. I promise. May my motherland forgive me for this!'

'Shree Eklingnathji Maharaj will bless every step,' Ajabde said, handing him his sword. 'Your decision to decentralise command and have smaller units spread across Mewar is a wise one. But please act swiftly—and keep this within your trusted circle until you have everyone's agreement.'

Pratap was leaving on an expedition to meet potential allies within and outside Mewar—rulers who were equally distrustful and indignant about the Mughals. Together, they would form a multi-pronged resistance. He knew it would still be no match to Akbar's strength—but it would shake him.

The Resistance

It would force him to reconsider his plans.

- *Rana Punja of Panwara (to meet)*
- *Dodia Bhim Singh of Lava (to meet)*
- *Raja Rama Shah and his sons of Gwalior (to meet)*
- *Hakim Khan Suri of the Sur dynasty (sent a letter, awaiting response)*

Amar Singh was rattling off names from the list his maiya and baapu had drawn up.

Pratap and Ajabde laughed. Amar Singh seemed just as engaged with the land and its future as Pratap had been as a child.

~

'Tej Lal! I see you're joining us,' Pratap said, pleased to find his friend waiting among the horsemen.

'Well, Maharanaji, I thought you'd never ask me to join you on an expedition,' Tej said with a shy smile. In their younger days, when Pratap was still Kunwar Pratap, they had joked freely. But now, with Pratap as Maharana, Tej didn't know how far he could go.

'Tej, my best men are coming with me—now and always. This is my closest friend, Bhura. I want both of you to reach out to your communities. Tell them we're planning

a resistance. We're inviting everyone to put their shoulder to the wheel. Everyone who has the spirit of independence burning within.'

The resistance had begun to take shape.

Yet the man in question—Akbar—had no interest in meeting Pratap head-on. He had understood by now that the Maharana had the immense support of his people and the clans around him. Jagmal, who had joined the Mughals, had sung like a canary. Akbar now knew every detail of Pratap's rise—even how his nobles had ousted Jagmal from the throne.

He knew that Pratap's bond with his land ran deep.

He would have to play this smart. Perhaps open a channel for negotiation?

Snubbed, c.1573

'You'll say what?' Ajabde looked at Pratap.

'You heard me, Maharani Ajabde,' Pratap replied, deliberately using the title to vex her.

'A stomach ache? Maharanaji, are you back to your boyhood? Man Singh is coming as the emissary of Akbar. I know this hasn't been officially announced, but it's more than evident. This would be a direct insult, and there's no saying what it could lead to.'

Ajabde wasn't fearful of battle—just of the immediacy of such a battle.

Fresh from defeating Rawal Askaran of Dungarpur, a close aide of Pratap, Man Singh had decided to meet the Maharana at his current residence in Udaipur. As he prepared for the meeting, he wondered how the interaction would unfold. *Saam, daam, dand, bhed*, he reminded himself.

MAHARANA PRATAP

He expected a cordial visit, in line with the strategy he had earlier proposed to Akbar.

But things didn't quite go as planned.

He was welcomed most warmly by Pratap, of course—after all, he was Amber's heir apparent. But when it came to dining together, the Maharana stepped away.

'Something seems to have disagreed with me, Kunwar Man Singh. I cannot take this meal with you. Kunwar Amar Singh will, of course, join you,' he said, gesturing to his son.

Man Singh looked at Pratap incredulously. *No attempt to even veil the insult!* he thought. *I understand the reason for the stomach ache only too well.*

But he didn't speak his mind. He had come, after all, to break the ice for more serious discussions about submission to Akbar. So, he masked his displeasure.

'I have come with the intention to meet Maharana Pratap, whose unmatched valour is spoken of across lands. I've come to dine with him. What is a little stomach ache compared to such friendship? Come, let's dine together.'

'Kunwar Man Singh, I had expected that an intelligent man like you would understand what has disagreed with me. Amar, please have the attendant bring Kunwar's plate,' Pratap said calmly.

That was quite enough.

'I know, Maharana Pratap. I understand very well. My aunt's marriage to Shahanshah Akbar is what has disagreed

Snubbed, c.1573

with you. But let me tell you this—if we have struck a matrimonial alliance with him, it is for the larger interest of protecting the people of Amber. But I think you're hardly interested in protecting anyone. You, in fact, seem eager to invite his ire,' Man Singh replied curtly. He refused to touch the food placed before him and left Udaipur in a huff.

Pratap knew he had triggered the lion. Man Singh would definitely strike back. But he was certain this was the only way he wanted to deal with Akbar and his emissaries.

'I want every single thing that this man touched—the ground he sat on, anything he may have made impure—purified completely. Dig up the soil and dispose of it. Throw away the plate, the bowl, the glass. I don't want my motherland to be defiled by any traces left by him,' Pratap thundered.

But, strangely, the lion didn't pounce.

Later that year, two more emissaries were sent. Bhagwant Das of Amber, Man Singh's father, came informally to speak to Pratap at Gogunda. And finally, Todar Mal from Akbar's court arrived with a formal proposal inviting him to be part of the Mughal empire.

Pratap had only one response for each of them: he showed them the door.

~

Akbar couldn't decide whether to be impressed by Pratap's refusal to bow or enraged by his defiance.

'Who, in their right senses, would choose the hardships of independence over my hand of friendship—with all the luxuries it offers?' he asked his council after Todar Mal returned with a straight and resounding *No*. 'This is not just a refusal. It's a show of complete disdain for the Mughal empire!'

He could feel his anger rising.

'It's his influence over the other Rajputs that worries me,' he admitted. Akbar had begun to feel the heat of Pratap's growing resistance.

He started flexing his muscles again. One by one, he targeted the smaller clans. But it felt like a game—no sooner had he defeated one chief than another rose in his place. When his army retreated for rest or supplies, they returned to find the rebellion alive again.

From Rao Chandra Sen, stationed in the Siwana hills, to Kunwar Kalla of Sojat, several Rajput chiefs were locked in battle with the Mughals.

Akbar had had enough.

He decided to fire his final salvo. He would step onto the battlefield himself, to witness the downfall of Mewar with his own eyes.

Snubbed, c.1573

'They are coming. News is that even Akbar may join the battle,' Bhamashah informed Pratap. His men had just returned with the update.

'How many?' Pratap asked, unflinching.

'At least five thousand.'

Haldighati, c.1576

'Must I wait and let the army enter? Must I surprise them by leading the army into their camp at nightfall? Must I lure them close to the pass?'

Sleep eluded Pratap that night before 21 June 1576.

Ajabde sat by his side. 'It is the moment you have been preparing for. You always knew that it will not be a fight of equal numbers, but where stature is concerned, we are in no way lesser than the Mughals. The difference is that we are fighting for our land and our independence, and they are fighting to take over our very identity.'

'Yes, but there are so many stakes involved. It is not just my fight, Ajabde.'

'It is, in fact, not your fight at all. You are leading the fight; you are the symbol of independence. You are someone who is standing unshakeable in the face of danger, someone

Haldighati, c.1576

who is not giving up when all the odds are stacked against you,' she said.

That was true. It was never the fight of one man against another; it was the fight of one thought against the other. 'Each one of those soldiers is following a thought, and that's keeping them going,' he realised. That gave him some calm and clarity about what was to be done. He smiled at his wife. 'Are you sure you've never been in battle before?'

Ajabde shook her head. 'I may not have been on the battlefield ever, but if I may say so, a tactical battle is what you must expect. You must have multiple plans. What if one fails?'

Akbar's army stood at Mandalgarh fort for two months – April and May. At its helm was not Akbar, as was earlier rumoured, but Man Singh. The Kachhwaha still seemed to be smarting from the insult dealt by Pratap during their earlier meet. Though Akbar was annoyed with him for not being able to negotiate a deal with Pratap earlier, he gave him charge with complete trust. But the same could not be said about Akbar's camp. There was a growing discontent against Man Singh.

'He is a Rajput; why will he defeat Pratap?'

'Our Jahaanpanah is too benevolent to give Man Singh the respect that he definitely does not deserve.'

Man Singh, however, knew better than to listen to the lower ranks. He was biding his time now, hoping he would be able to tempt Pratap to come to the plains. But the Mughal army was getting weary of the wait.

'Why don't we snuff him out of the hole!' shouted Sayyad Ahmad Khan Barha one day, entering Man Singh's tent. Ahmad Khan, Akbar's renowned general, was to hold the right wing in the battle.

'I want him to move out of his secure hills,' Man Singh roared in exasperation.

'How difficult can it be to directly attack him? This is the Mughal army we are talking of, Man Singh, not some small local clan,' argued Ahmad Khan in a condescending tone.

That was a direct attack on his Kachhwaha clan and Man Singh didn't take it kindly.

'How difficult, Ahmad Khan? This is Pratap we are talking about, not some rabbit you can "snuff out of some hole" and leap on to. Have you looked around you? This is the grand Aravalli. You don't just get through by force; there has to be a strategy in place. This is precisely why Jahaanpanah has selected me to lead in this battle. I know the region and the people. The sooner all of us digest that, the better.'

Haldighati, c.1576

'Tej, what news do you bring?' Pratap asked his trusted friend and the fastest horseman in his army. Their contingent had moved out from Kumbhalgarh and was headed to Khamnur village.

'They are at Molela, Maharanaji, not very far from here. The plan is to stay there till they understand the surrounding area. They've sent out their horseman for an overview. Even a large army such as theirs will not take too long to reach Haldighati,' he reported.

'Keeka, we must let them come to the pass. We will crush them!' he said, clenching his fists.

Rawat Sanga, the seniormost statesman and warrior, watched as the young bloods were raring to go.

'And you are naïve enough to believe that Man Singh will let his men come to Haldighati in spite of fully understanding the danger it holds for them?' he said. 'He most definitely won't.'

'Rawat Sangaji is correct. From experience, we can tell you that we will have to draw them into battle in the open and bring them into the pass in the heat of the battle. Akbar has rightly put Man Singh in charge of the force. He knows the land only too well. But the size of his army—what we think is his biggest strength—is also his weakness. The massive army is slow to move. Moreover, they have a poor understanding of the region,' Rawat Kishandas added.

Just then Bhamashah came rushing to the camp with an opportunity that was supremely tempting.

'Maharanaji! We have news. Man Singh has just left for a hunting expedition. He is accompanied by only a thousand men.'

Keeka and Tej immediately spoke up. 'Let's get him!'

Rawat Sanga and Rawat Kishandas were also in agreement.

'This is an opportunity. If we launch a night attack, then we will decimate his troops in no time. The battle will be over before it has even started,' said Rawat Kishandas.

'But will it be right? Will it be an ethical thing for the Maharana of Mewar to do?'

It was an old chief of Pratap, Man Singh Jhala, also known as Jhala Bida.

The wait was excruciatingly long but Man Singh was certain he didn't want to be tempted into the Haldighati pass.

'Pilgrims have used it while going to Makkah. It is flanked by huge mountains on either side and it can barely hold two horseback riders at one go. Haldighati will be a death trap for my men and will be the cause of certain defeat for us,' thought Man Singh.

'We wait!' he hollered to his men once again.

Haldighati, c.1576

The soldiers were having a tough time. The blazing hot Mewar sun made them uneasy and the wait even more so. Moreover, Pratap's scorched earth policy had hit them hard. There was a scarcity of water and no fresh crop which could be used to boost food reserves.

Man Singh was hoping the impasse would soon be broken. Thankfully for him, Pratap decided to make the first move.

'I want the Bhil army led by Bhura to be positioned at Haldighati. We will meet Man Singh very close to the pass and attack with all our might,' announced Pratap to his team.

Rawat Sanga explained the battle formation.

'Hakim Khan Suriji, you will lead our front guard along with Rawat Kishandasji, Dodia Bhim Singhji, Rawat Ramdasji and me. Maharanaji, of course, will be at the centre with Bhamashahji, Tarachandji and Bhura. Raja Ram Singhji Tomar—you and your sons, Kunwar Shalivahan, Kunwar Pratap and Kunwar Bhavani—will form the right flank of the army. Jhala Bidaji, you will command the left flank. The rear will be brought up by Rana Punjaji and Tej, along with the Bhil archers.'

Pratap addressed his commanders and soldiers.

'My friends! What I see here is not just immense hatred for the invaders. I see a selfless love for our motherland. I see the vision of securing our future by giving up our present. I see entire families giving up their lives for this insurmountable challenge. What will come out of this? I don't know. But this much I do know—our freedom is not for sale. Our motherland is our pride! And for her, we will not leave any stone unturned! *Jai Mewar! Jai Vaagdevi! Jai Shree Eklingnathji!*'

Each of them held up their swords and their bows and arrows. The air was thick with the cries of 'Jai Mewar! Jai Vaagdevi! Jai Shree Eklingnathji!'

Chetak's Leap of Faith

MAN SINGH WAS ALLOCATING ROLES TO HIS COMMANDERS. His uncle, Jagannath Kachhwaha, was to lead from the front, with a portion of the soldiers led by Sayyad Hashim—especially earmarked to ward off any surprise attacks that the Mewari army was infamous for. The left flank was to be manned by Ghazi Khan Badakshani and Rao Loonkaran. Sayyad Ahmad Khan Barha would bring up the right flank, while the rear would be handled by Mahtar Khan.

Just before daybreak on 21 June 1576, Jagannath Kachhwaha felt mighty uneasy. He went up to his nephew, Man Singh.

'Uneasy, *tau sa*? Why? It's not the first battle you've fought,' Man Singh reacted.

'It's not the unease before a war, Man. It's an unsettling feeling before this particular one,' replied the older Kachhwaha general. 'This feels like I am fighting against my own blood. Worse still, it feels like I am in cahoots with the enemy and have betrayed my own land,' he continued, quite inconsolable.

Man Singh could not meet his eyes. He knew that feeling too. It had taken over his being ever since the day he returned from Udaipur after being snubbed by Pratap. But he couldn't afford to dwell on the ethical question—not now, when they were on the brink of war. A lot was at stake.

The Mewar army came charging at Man Singh's troops. For the first time, the Mughal army was shocked at the vigour with which they were attacked. Maybe it was the pent-up anger from all the jauhars and sakas that Mewar's history had witnessed. Maybe it was the shared agony of constantly living under the threat of foreign rule. Maybe they had nothing to lose in this fight. Whatever it was, it gave the Mewaris an upper hand right at the beginning of the battle.

The Mughal front guard crumbled under their crushing force. The left flank was dismantled too. Man Singh's soldiers began to flee from the field and move towards the camp.

Pratap kept surging ahead on Chetak, who was made to wear the mask of an elephant to deceive the Mughal elephants. Bhura had told Pratap, 'Keeka, elephants never attack their young ones. If Chetak appears like a young elephant, there is very little chance of the other elephants stopping him. You can easily get close to Man Singh then.'

Chetak's Leap of Faith

Reaching Man Singh—positioned right in the centre of the field—was Pratap's sole focus.

As swords met swords and blood painted the landscape of Rakt Talai, Pratap and his men slayed enemy generals. The Maharana also had a keen eye on the happenings around him. Everything was going according to plan. His Bhil army had by now started crushing Man Singh's forces by throwing huge boulders on them. From their vantage position on either side of the narrow pass of Haldighati, they shot down hundreds with their arrows. There was chaos in the Mughal camp. They ran for their lives.

Pratap seemed satisfied. The outcome looked completely in their favour—but they couldn't afford to be lax. They had to take this fight to the finish.

Mahtar Khan was waiting for his turn to strike. He had to bring up the rear of the formation. But what he observed on the battlefield alarmed him beyond measure. Their army was in complete disarray. He had to do something—something that would rouse his soldiers, who seemed defeated in spirit.

'Bring in the drummers and trumpeters! Now! Let it be known that the Shahanshah has joined us in battle against Pratap,' he ordered his chief.

'B-but how can we do this? He isn't here! The men will feel let down,' the chief replied.

'I don't care. We need something drastic to change this game! And we need it right now!' he shouted.

The drums started beating, the trumpets hooting. Mahtar Khan's strategy turned the tables against the Mewaris. Just as he had thought, the mere possibility of Akbar being with them energised the army. The soldiers began to rally together and fight back.

Tej galloped to Pratap. 'Maharanaji, it is a ploy! Akbar is not here. I have confirmation of this!'

Pratap was furious. He couldn't let the situation get out of hand. Having spotted Man Singh, he patted Chetak.

'Chetak, my brother, my friend! We need to do this. It's now or never.'

Chetak knew exactly what needed to be done. Off the battlefield, he and Pratap had practised this multiple times.

Fast as lightning, he flew right up to the elephant on which Man Singh sat, taking the elephant, the mahout and the commander—all by surprise. Pratap was now within attacking distance of Man Singh, and he flung his spear at him. Man Singh was lucky. He ducked, and the spear went through the mahout instead.

But Pratap had tasted blood, and he steadied himself for his next assault. Man Singh was utterly shocked at how Pratap had pulled this off. Seeing that Pratap was readying

Chetak's Leap of Faith

for another strike, he began to steer his elephant away from the centre. By now, Man Singh's generals had seen that their commander was in trouble and started galloping towards him to form a safety net.

Pratap pulled out his sword and lunged forward, patting Chetak once more. But something was amiss. Chetak neighed out in pain. That's when Pratap noticed it. The damage had been done.

In the attack on Man Singh, Chetak's right leg had been deeply wounded by a sword that was tied to the trunk of Man Singh's elephant. Pratap had always thought of Chetak as his unshakeable source of power. He remembered how he had first had a vision of a flying horse in his dreams as a young boy. To see him grievously wounded was unthinkable. Visibly shaken, Pratap continued to ward off enemy soldiers. He suffered a gash across his leg and one on his arm.

Bhura, Bhamashah, and Jhala Bida had simultaneously witnessed the fall of Chetak—and its effect on Pratap. Man Singh's men were closing in on him all at once. The Maharana was slaying his way through, breaking their stranglehold, but he needed support.

Bhura was the first to be by his side.

'Keeka, it is time for our alternate plan! Move away!!' he said, slashing an attacking sword away from Pratap. He looked straight at him. 'Don't stop. Don't look back.

Chetak's Leap of Faith

As many as can return to you, will return,' he said, before disappearing into the crowd of swords, spears and arrows.

Swiftly, Jhala Bida was by Pratap's side. He took his place under the Mewar canopy.

'Go off, Maharanaji! I promise not to fail you. Just like my ancestor, Raja Ajja Jhala, had taken the place of Maharana Sanga, so shall I take your place. Jai Mewar!!' he said, before plunging back into the battle.

With his trusted Chetak injured, Pratap had only one route to follow.

It was now the Mughal army's turn to be deceived. They closed in on Jhala Bida, assuming they had Pratap—unaware that the bird had flown the coop. Jhala Bida's last words rang through the air: 'Jai Mewar!'

~

Chetak had one final burst left in him.

Ahead lay a stream. In his prime, he would have crossed it with ease. But now, every step was a battle. His leg throbbed. He winced.

But Pratap was hurt. He needed safety.

Chetak would get him there.

He stepped back three paces, steadying himself.

Then, he ran.

The Aftermath

'WILL WE LEAVE WITHOUT BAAPU?' AMAR SINGH ASKED HIS mother. 'Why can't I go to Haldighati instead? I am old enough to bear the wounds of war!' She simply wouldn't reply.

Guru Avadhuta took Amar aside. 'You are just like your father,' he smiled. 'Just like I had explained to him once, I will tell you too. Sometimes the final cause is far greater than what you see in the short term. You are required in the future for greater things, Kunwar Amar. So, please go ahead and follow that path.'

Then he bade Gogunda's villagers and the royal family farewell and stood by with a band of 40 soldiers to defend Gogunda from the attackers, if need be. 'They will definitely come here to exploit the loot of war,' he thought.

Ajabde took his blessings and turned to her family. 'Tej Lalji is Maharanaji's trusted friend. He has come to help us

The Aftermath

move immediately out of Gogunda. We will proceed in the direction of Zawar. There will be no stops and not a single word whispered till I permit you to do so. No questions asked. Lakhiji Meena from Zawar has come to take us to his caves,' she commanded.

~

'Are you fools? How could you have mistaken one of his generals for Pratap?' Ahmad Khan was livid at the generals and soldiers who had attacked and slain Jhala Bida.

'Ahmad Khan! This is part of war tactics. Mahtar Khan announced that Jahaanpanah was joining us in war; they used a trick too,' Man Singh shouted back.

Pratap was nowhere to be found. The Mughals were as badly injured as the Mewari soldiers. Bodies lay slashed everywhere across Haldighati and Rati Talai. After Pratap's sudden disappearance, his commanders had followed suit. The Mughal soldiers were too tired and defeated in spirit to give them a chase.

'Okay, agreed. But we must comb the area, Man Singh! Now is our chance! We have the upper hand,' Ahmad Khan reasoned.

'Upper hand? Us? Yes, we were two to one and we couldn't capture him,' Man Singh sighed. 'We won't follow Pratap. It won't be of any use.' The Mughal generals around him were

aghast to hear that command. Man Singh took a while to think, then announced, 'We will lay siege to Gogunda. If we capture it, at least there will be some evidence of us having had the upper hand, as you call it, Ahmad Khan.'

Ahmad Khan glared.

∼

Rawat Kishandas had seen several ups and downs in his life. But what had happened in these past few days had affected him deeply. A valiant young Pratap had made a near-impossible attempt to defeat Man Singh. The Mughal army had held its ground but the Mewari army had managed to get under its skin. Sadly, the Mewaris couldn't claim success but, thankfully, neither could the Mughals. Reports of the growing discontent for Man Singh were trickling out of the Mughal camp. Gogunda had been captured but Pratap was out, still on the prowl, leaving the Mughals uneasy. His confidante and friend, Rawat Sanga, had been martyred, Pratap's trusted Chetak was no more, and scores of other kings and soldiers had given up their lives.

Being among the most experienced people in the team, it was his responsibility to rally the men around. 'Jai Mewar!' he said, fist up in the air. The Kolyari forest echoed with cries of 'Jai Mewar'.

The Aftermath

'I am proud of each one of you who fought at Haldighati! We gave the Mughals a fight that they will remember for generations to come,' he said.

Pratap sat with his remaining men. His wounds were healing, as were those of the others; but he had suffered personal losses, the wounds of which would never heal. He stood up. 'Rawat Kishandasji, I am grateful for the way you have rallied the men and arranged to bring them all to Kolyari. Bhura, you saved my life on the battlefield. Bhamashahji and Tarachandji, you have always been with Mewar. Tej, it was your plan to alert Lakhi and take the royal family to safety in Zawar. I have a lot to be thankful for. I can thank all of you who are here,' he paused. 'But I am proud of all who are not here. And I can say this, we will not forget, we will not let them forget,' he said, his voice rising. '*Chetak ki jai! Rawat Sanga ki jai! Jhala Bida ki jai! Jai Mewar!*'

'Jai Mewar!' came the resounding reply.

'Maharanaji, our policy of scorching the crops and shutting the wells has worked excellently. The Mughals may have got Gogunda but their resources are dwindling and they have had to resort to killing their horses for meat,' said Bhamashah.

'Hmm. What news about Mughals looking for us? Bhura?'

'Nothing, Keeka. Looks like the Rajput blood in Man Singh has finally had its effect. He has told his generals not to chase us. I hear from the soldiers that Akbar is not at all happy with

The Aftermath

Man Singh. There is also some chatter about Akbar himself marching on to Mewar,' Bhura replied. 'My men will keep a lookout but we must keep changing our spots.'

'We must, yes. Tej, I would like you to reach Zawar—it isn't too far from here—and thank Lakhi Meena. Then I would like you to tell Maharani Ajabde that she should arrange for all the queens and children to take a safe route back to their maternal homes. Request Lakhi to help them,' Pratap instructed.

'Yes, Maharanaji. But what if Maharani Ajabde and Kunwar Amar wish to join you?' Tej hesitantly asked.

'They have to go to Bijolia, Tej. Look around you. We are living in caves and on trees in thick forests. We don't have enough to eat at times. How will she or Amar stay here? It is a ridiculous thought! What made you even think of this?' Pratap snapped.

'When we were leaving Gogunda, Kunwar Amar refused to leave. He wanted to fight.'

The anger melted away from Pratap's face.

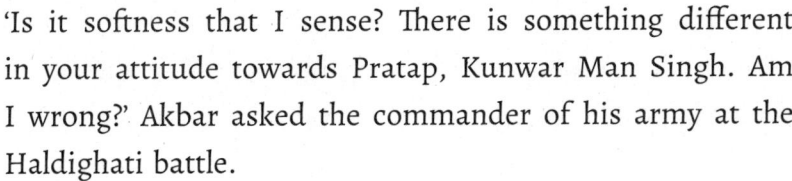

'Is it softness that I sense? There is something different in your attitude towards Pratap, Kunwar Man Singh. Am I wrong?' Akbar asked the commander of his army at the Haldighati battle.

'Pardon me, Jahaanpanah, for my saying so, but there is no softening of my stance whatsoever. Unless someone has reported things wrongly to you,' Man Singh cast a glance at Ahmad Khan.

'We had him but we didn't. We got the fort but we ran out of provisions. Then we left the fort too! Aren't there too many coincidences here to be neglected?' Akbar said, with a tinge of sarcasm. 'I suggest, Kunwar Man Singh, that you take a break from the Mughal court for a while. The battle has done you no good.'

Man Singh nodded. *And this is what I left my Amber for*, he thought.

~

The game was afoot. Pratap and Akbar were equals in terms of strategy and their devotion to their legacy.

Pratap was leading by example in all of Rajputana. Not many could have thought of leading a much smaller army against the might of the Mughals and giving them a challenging time in the battlefield. Consequently, every ruler with an iota of self-respect in him had risen in rebellion—Raja Narain Das of Idar, Rao Surtan of Sarohi, Taj Khan of Jalore and Rao Chander Sen of Jodhpur. Each of them was supported by the Maharana of Mewar.

The Aftermath

But it wasn't too difficult for Akbar to quell such rebellions. Through force or through promises, he managed to break away these rulers from Pratap, with the exception of Rao Chander Sen of Jodhpur.

It was like a game of chess. If Pratap got back Gogunda from Man Singh's army, Akbar soon captured it again. If Akbar sent out forces with confirmed news of Pratap being present in Kumbhalgarh fort, his men would return mysteriously empty-handed. Whether they spread their web of spies and soldiers across the region or cut off the routes that Pratap frequented, the Mughals just could not get hold of him. Pratap, on the other hand, had a new policy that worked brilliantly for him. He would give up his bastion without resistance but would recapture it once the Mughal guard was down.

'This can't be. My pilgrims to Mecca pass through Mewar and I don't want them to be unsafe,' Akbar shouted in frustration. Shahbaz Khan listened on. As Akbar's head of military, he knew that the Shahanshah's concern was not unfounded. Pratap's attacks were sudden, his fleet of soldiers nimble, and his network of Bhils dangerous. 'I will personally go after him and finish this resistance once and for all, Shahanshah,' he promised.

Man Singh and his father, Bhagwant Das, were assigned by Akbar as his assistants in the Mewar region. But while Shahbaz wanted to destroy the lands of Mewar wherever

he didn't find Pratap, both the Rajputs were reluctant to do so. Shahbaz was ruthless; he sent the duo marching back to Ajmer while he continued onward.

∼

'Maharanaji, he is destroying anything that comes his way. There is open loot. Villages are being plundered, forts conquered. There is no stopping him.' Bhamashah spoke gravely.

'Sending Shahbaz Khan in our pursuit only means that Akbar is getting unsettled. That's a good sign, Bhamashahji. We won't attack and make ourselves visible to him. We don't want any damage done to our army and resources. Let's lie low. He will either get happy too soon, or tired of hunting us down. When he stops, it will be our turn,' said Pratap. Standing near him, Bhura smiled.

The game continued with Shahbaz Khan too. He captured Kumbhalgarh, Gogunda and Udaipur. Almost simultaneously, Pratap attacked Mughal posts from his mountainous hideouts and looted their supplies.

Fed up of these mixed stories of losses and victories emanating from Mewar, Akbar appointed Abdul Rahim Khan-i-Khana—also known as poet Rahim, and son of his guardian Bairam Khan—to govern Ajmer. Rahim Khan's additional, and more important, task was to capture Pratap.

The Man Behind the Maharana, 1578–1584

'AJABDE, TILL LAST MONTH I HAD NO IDEA HOW WE WOULD sustain the troops and our family. And now, by the blessings of Shree Eklingnathji Maharaj, doesn't the treasury look better? All thanks to Bhamashahji and Tarachandji.' Pratap was sitting with his queen on the floor in one of the caves in Zawar. 'Bhamashahji has not only been a brave warrior but also a trustworthy prime minister.'

Ajabde nodded. 'They have gifted Mewar a new lease of life with this money and gold coins. And to plunder Akbar's posts in Malwa! It requires character.'

'We can take back Kumbhalgarh now, Ajabde, and get back our home,' he said, looking around. 'Living in these mines is not something I wanted for you or the children. To fight with Akbar has been my destiny, but these hardships for my family were not something I had bargained for.'

'What can I say?' smiled Ajabde. 'A partnership for life is not for the faint-hearted!'

The two of them burst out laughing. It had been a long time since they had sat together and laughed thus. It reminded them of their days in Udaipur and Gogunda and Kumbhalgarh.

Pratap's thoughts went back to his childhood days. 'You know, it's ironic how you make kodo ki roti for us now. Listen to the stories Bhura has about these! His maiya had fed me these grass rotis once and said I'd never be able to feast on such rotis again. If she were alive, she would've been surprised to know what I had for lunch today!' A deep sense of despair suddenly came over him. 'But Ajabde, to see our children grow up like this is painful. They are born into a royal family but live a life that has none of the fancy luxuries of royalty.'

Ajabde held his hand. 'Hardship only builds character. They must know how the others in their kingdom live. Nobody said the path you decided to take would be easy. But this is the only path. The right path. We agree on that.'

~

Rahim Khan was flabbergasted. His post in Sherpura had been ravaged by Pratap's son, Amar, while he was out on an expedition. The whole area was in ruins and his entire family

The Man Behind the Maharana, 1578-1584

was missing. 'He has taken them, huzoor!' his right-hand man came to give him the devastating news.

~

'Kunwar Amar Singh! Is this what you have learnt from your father, from all your ancestors?' Pratap glared at his son. Amar knew at once that what he had done was not ethical. But in the euphoria of capturing the Mughal post of Sherpura, taking Rahim's family as prisoners had been the first thing that had occurred to him. The women and children now stood before the Maharana, murmuring their final prayers. After all, everyone knew what happened to those caught in the crossfire of war.

'I want you to send them back to their home with complete dignity and security,' Pratap declared.

The family had never heard anything like this before. When they returned, not only was Rahim relieved but also completely won over by the very man he was meant to capture. The poet went so far as to write a couplet on Pratap:

All is unstable in this world,
Land and wealth will disappear,
But the virtue of a great name lives forever.
Pratap abandoned wealth and land,
But never bowed the head.

Alone of all the princes of Hind,
He preserved the honour of his race.

~

It was the ninth night of Navratri when Pratap marched towards Dewair. 'Rawat Kishandasji, isn't it strange that we aren't home for Shastra Puja on Dussehra this year?' Along with the senior warrior and Amar Singh by his side, the Maharana wanted to spring a huge surprise attack on the unsuspecting Mughal army.

'For a warrior, Maharanaji, war, and the promise of victory itself should be puja, I think,' replied Rawat Kishandas.

It was to be a night of resounding successes.

Dewair, an important Mughal post, was commanded by Sultan Khan. The Mughal soldiers were caught unawares by the sudden attack, and when their leader was struck down by Amar Singh, they fled the field.

Bolstered by the victory, Pratap made for his home, Kumbhalgarh, devastating every Mughal post en route. Having captured Kumbhalgarh, his army swiftly moved to Zawar, capturing Mughal posts all the way.

Building on these successes, Pratap kept pushing forward and either regained or won over new territories. The Chhappan area to the south of Udaipur, the Chawand

The Man Behind the Maharana, 1578-1584

area south of Mewar, Dungarpur, and Banswara came under his rule.

The map of Mewar was changing. It had taken a decade since Pratap was crowned the ruler, and it had been an excruciatingly painful process, but the results had begun to show.

That same year, Jagmal, Pratap's fugitive brother, was killed in a skirmish.

'Jagmal daada has been killed, Daada! By Rao Surtan! We must avenge his death,' Sagar Singh urged his eldest brother. Sagar was Jagmal's younger brother, born to Dheer Bai.

'Sagar, much as I feel for a fellow Sisodia brother having met such a violent death, you must understand that Jagmal interfered with the peace of the Surtans of Sarohi. He faced the consequences of his actions,' said Pratap, rather matter-of-factly.

'But I hear that you're thinking of getting our Kesar Kanwarji married to him. That can't be! He has killed my brother—our brother.' Sagar was aghast.

'Kesar is Amar's daughter. A valiant warrior like Rao Surtan will be a suitable match for her,' replied Pratap.

One thing Pratap was certain of was that he didn't want personal enmity to come in the way of building new collaborations for Mewar and retaining her independence.

He paid a high price. Yet another brother defected to the Akbar camp.

~

'Raja Jagannathji Kachhwaha, I place a lot of expectations on you. Go and get me Pratap—something none of my earlier commanders have been able to do. And that list includes your brother, Bhagwant Das, and your nephew, Man Singh.'

Akbar was tired of sending expeditions and spending enormous resources with no final outcome. His war with Mewar had continued for almost 20 years. Pratap had been a thorn in his flesh for nearly 15 of those 20 years. There was helplessness in his demeanour. He wanted results now—or he wanted out.

Destiny had the second option in mind.

Peace for Mewar, c.1585

'We have a home again, Ajabde. Do you like it?'

'It's perfect for us to grow old in, Maharanaji,' said his queen. 'But I must admit, it doesn't look very different from a military camp!'

Pratap smiled. Years of fighting the Mughals had drilled into him the necessity of building hideouts. He had built his capital at Chawand, a little distance away from his father's dream home, Udaipur, towards the south of Mewar. It had at least a dozen hideouts in its 10-kilometre periphery—perfect spaces for his weaponry, his forces, and even the warriors of his Bhil community. 'Well, let me just say that it was Bhura's idea.'

'Ah! Of course, it was!' laughed Ajabde. 'So, after so many years of fighting for Mewar, have you figured out if winning is all that really matters?' she asked, turning to Pratap. 'Years ago, you had asked Guru Avadhutaji this.'

'Yes, and he had said that it depends on what your idea of victory is,' Pratap replied, picking up his grandson, Karan, who had come running to him.

It was a unique feeling—to live the life that he had earned. To live in the knowledge that there was an Akbar somewhere who had come to understand that he had underestimated the might of this Maharana. Yes, Pratap could lament that he still didn't have Chittor back—but the road ahead was still long. There was no giving up.

Importantly, most of Mewar was his again, and Pratap could now divert his attention beyond military expeditions and battles to administration, academics, and the arts. He had nurtured many artists and musicians. Nasiruddin, an artist who explored what came to be called the Chawand Ragmala paintings, was one of them. He could spend time with the three-year-old Karan, Amar's son. Finally, there was an opportunity for everyone to come together and enjoy market days, fairs, festivals, and community entertainment in the town square. Mewar was alive once more.

'The Chamunda Mataji temple is magnificent, Maharanaji. She is a warrior goddess!' Ajabde said, bringing him back to the present.

'You had asked me once what I thought of women. You had also said that women are rarely acknowledged. Do you remember? I wish we can change that completely someday,' Pratap said.

Ajabde smiled.

'So, you seem to have taken care of everything that we had often spoken of. However, there is one promise that still remains to be fulfilled. Do you remember which one?' she asked him.

'I was wondering when you would ask,' came the quick reply. 'I have something for you to see.' He took her to the room that housed the many books that he finally had time to read.

'Here is *Vishwa Vallabh* that Chakrapani Misraji has written. He has taken a lot of effort to find out how to recognise the best soil, how to detect the sources of water, how to support vegetation, how to preserve soil, how to purify hard and salty water, how to...'

Ajabde's eyes widened in surprise. 'Hey Eklingnathji Maharaj! Are you a warrior, Maharanaji? Or a farmer in disguise?'

'Warrior or farmer, you wonder, Maharani Ajabde? My mother used to call me a dreamer. And a dreamer, I am.'

Acknowledgements

For this book, I have relied not just on factual information on Maharana Pratap but also on folklore that I had heard from my travels in Mewar some years ago. So, while I have a few books and authors to mention here, there are scores of unknown voices that I can only thank in spirit. I picked up two books, written almost a century apart, to guide me through this journey–Rima Hooja's *Maharana Pratap: The Invincible Warrior* (2019) and Sri Ram Sharma's *Maharana Pratap* (1930).

However, the beauty of historical fiction is in how we writers get to imagine the worlds of the past, the people who lived then, and what might have guided their actions. Weaving that narrative is a beautiful exercise, and I must thank Vidhi Bhargava for entrusting me with the job.

I am grateful to my wonderful illustrator, Charbak Dipta, who grounded this narrative in realistic illustrations.

ACKNOWLEDGEMENTS

To my editors, Arpita Dasgupta and Muhammed Lesin, who undoubtedly have microscopic lenses fitted into their very being, a big thank you.

A truckload of gratitude to my inner circle: My husband, Jagdish, and my son, Krishang, who did not once suspect me of having lost my marbles as I enacted my scenes at the work desk, my mother, who stands solid as a rock behind me through all my emotional breakdowns, and my partner-in-crime, Anjana Nagabhushana, who is very patient and goes through each of my manuscripts saying that someday she will extract her pound of flesh.